EASTER DECODED: JESUS'S EVERLASTING MIRACLE OF THE EARTHLY STAGES OF HUMAN CREATION

The New Gospel Revelations Series 2

The New Gospel Revelations Series *of* the New
Christianity of Christ Essentials Made Easy. *The Words
and Works of Christ Decoded*

Festus Enumah M.D.

The New Gospel Revelations Series of the New Christianity of Christ *Essentials* Made
Easy
The Words and Works of Jesus Christ Decoded
Easter Decoded: Jesus's Everlasting Miracle of the Earthly Stages of Human Creation
The New Gospel Revelations Series 2
Copyright © 2016
Authored by Festus Enumah M.D.
All rights reserved

For information regarding permission, write to:
Festus Enumah, M.D.
1629 10th Avenue. Columbus. GA 31901. USA

The Library of Congress of United States in Cataloging
Festus Enumah M.D
1629 10th Avenue. Columbus, Georgia, 31901. USA
ISBN: 0692753907
ISBN 13: 9780692753903
Library of Congress Control Number: 2016911436
Festus Enumah, Columbus, GA

DEDICATION

This book is dedicated to:
Jesus Christ who used Himself as a model in the everlasting miracle of human creation.

Other books by Festus Enumah M.D.

The Innocent Blood and Judas Iscariot
The Father's Business and the Spiritual Cross

Coming soon.
Complete Volume (The New *Gospel* Revelations Series 1-5) *of* the
New Christianity of Christ
Essentials Made Easy. *The Words and Works of Jesus Christ Decoded*
The New *Gospel* Revelations Series1–The Naked Truth: Jesus's
Kingdom of God and its Mysteries decoded
The New *Gospel* Revelations Series 3- ABC's of Eternal Life and
Jesus's Role in Human Creation
The New *Gospel* Revelations Series 4-The Mysteries of Golgotha:
Why Jesus Died
The New Revelations Series 5-*An Exemplary Christian: German
Chancellor Angela Merkel. **What makes you *NOT* a Christian.

CONTENTS

Introduction   ix

Chapter 1   Initiation of Jesus's Everlasting Miracle
             of the Earthly Stages of Human Creation   1
Chapter 2   Jesus and the Spiritualization of Human Souls   14
Chapter 3   The Director of the Miracle: God,
             the Father of Jesus Christ   27
Chapter 4   Provocative Acts of Jesus Directed Against
             Jewish and Roman Authorities   38
Chapter 5   Jesus's Trial and Condemnation to Death
             by the Jewish Authorities   54
Chapter 6   Jesus Allowed the Romans to Crucify Him   69
Chapter 7   Jesus Died as a Human Being at Golgotha   72
Chapter 8   The Mysteries of Jesus's Resurrection Revealed   76
Chapter 9   The New Easter Experience and the
             Triumphant Glory of Jesus's Kingdom   85
Chapter 10   Post-Resurrection Scenes of
             Jesus's Miracle of Life   94
Chapter 11   Ascension of Christ at Bethany,
             near Mount Olives   98

Chapter 12   The Promised Gift of the Holy Spirit
              of Christ and Pentecost   100

Bibliography   113
About the Author   119

INTRODUCTION

To this end was I born, and for this cause came I unto the world.

—Jesus

The most important thing that happened two thousand years ago in Palestine and is still happening right now was what Jesus demonstrated in His epic miracle of the earthly stages of human creation. In executing that miracle, Jesus used Himself as a model that gave proof, beyond what any scientific methods could provide, of what He came to accomplish: revelation of His Father and Himself, public demonstration of the creative power of the Spirit of His Father, knowledge of who we are, why we are here as humans, and His Father's plan for all mankind. By utilizing the infinite power of His Kingdom of God (the Spirit of the Father in Him), Jesus gave a public display of the proof of the divine authenticity of His origin and all His words and works that originated from a living true God, He called His Father. In doing so, Jesus allowed us to glimpse into His spiritual world and that of His Father. It was for the demonstration and execution of that miracle that Jesus was sent into this world as a human being, by His Father. If Jesus's humanity was removed from that epic miracle, the significance of the miracle itself and its mysteries would remain hidden.

For the same reason, Jesus Christ had the Spirit of His Father in His human soul as we all do through Him.

The epic miracle incorporated the entire spectrum of the works Jesus was given by His Father. All the words and works of Jesus bore the trademark of that miracle and the divine element Jesus used for its accomplishment. That divine element is Jesus's Kingdom of God. The earthly visible phase of that work was finished at Golgotha. The spiritual phase started with His proclamation of the Kingdom of God, manifested on the third day after His death with His resurrection and subsequently with the promised gift of His risen glorified Holy Spirit that was bestowed on the apostles on the day of Pentecost, when the final scene of that miracle was revealed. Jesus used Himself as a model. It was an extraordinary everlasting miracle that comprised the three stages of the earthly phases in human creation and started with Jesus's proclamation of His Kingdom of God. That miracle was portrayed in the following miraculous Acts:

> Act 1 the demonstration—in miracles—of the power of the Kingdom of God in Him (the Spirit of the Father in Him) in cities and villages in Palestine
> Act 2 the crucifixion and the death of Jesus at Golgotha
> Act 3a His resurrection at the tomb site where He was buried.
> Act 3b the promised gift of His glorified Holy Spirit to the apostles that came on the day of Pentecost.

The comprehension of Jesus's miracle of the earthly stages of human creation is the key that unlocks the mysteries of His Kingdom of God and revealed all His words and works. That miracle was "the Light that shined in darkness; and the darkness comprehended it not." (John 1:5). It was the light that revealed, in essence, why Jesus was born as a human being and why His Father sent Him to this world. It was the light that revealed all the mysteries of Golgotha and the mysteries of Jesus's Kingdom of God.

What ended at Golgotha was the beginning of Jesus's earthly performances of the final stage of that miracle that was made manifest by His resurrection and subsequently by the promised gift of His glorified Holy Spirit that came on the day of Pentecost. The performances gave an audience the opportunity to see and interact with the risen Christ on the third day and witnessed His ascension forty days later. Many were still in Jerusalem and witnessed the final scene of the miracle that was revealed on the day of Pentecost. The Christians rejoiced and called the resurrection of Christ a miracle. It was, indeed a miracle, and formed the very foundation of the Christian Faith. However, what we celebrate as Easter today is only the result of a scene in the third and final stage of Jesus's miracle of human creation. What was handed down to us was incomplete vision of the entire spectrum of that epic miracle. It was for this reason that the true meaning of Easter was difficult to comprehend. What Jesus's three staged miracle revealed, remains hidden to us. Additionally, our inability to identify the divine element, the power of His Kingdom of God that Jesus used in that miracle became an obstacle, not only in understanding that miracle but also in finding ourselves in it.

My dear reader, do not blame yourself. Though many people in cities and villages across Palestine and at Golgotha witnessed that timeless miracle, its interpretation at that time was kept secret by Christ and His Father. Why did Jesus, the miracle worker, who performed more than forty recorded miracles, refused to reveal the meaning of what He was doing at various stages that epic miracle? Why did He not call His death and resurrection a miracle? Jesus simply refused to reveal to the people that He was going to use the power of the Kingdom of God to perform a miracle and used Himself as a model to demonstrate the earthly stages of human creation. In fact, Jesus did not call any of His works "miracles." It is the Christians who call some of them miracles. Jesus went about the cities and villages in Palestine performing miracles and no one noticed that He was at the same time initiating the performance of once upon a time epic three-part miracle of human life. For the last two thousand years, we failed to recognize all the segments of that epic miracle. We failed to recognize the exemplary of the human creative activities in the death and resurrection of Christ. We relegated what happened on the day of Pentecost to the apostles. We did not see ourselves in any of those events. What was delivered to us was to hope for life after death. How could we have missed all the vital information the miracle provided? Why was Jesus silent on its meaning? Because of His silence, the full interpretation of His words and works appeared to become impossible frontiers.

If I with the finger of God cast out devils, no doubt the Kingdom of God is come upon you.

---Jesus. Luke 11:20

Believest thou not that I am in the Father, and the Father in me? The words that I speak unto you I speak not of myself: but the Father that dwelleth in me, he doeth the works.

---Jesus. John 14:10

The finger of God is the metaphor for the Spirit of His Father. As Jesus openly revealed, the invisible Spirit of the Father powered all of His words and works and is the core element in His Kingdom of God. Jesus's ability to heal the dumb man (Luke 11:14) revealed that power. Jesus showed the power of His kingdom of God by performing many other miracles, as well. In essence, all His miracles—of healing, controlling nature, feeding five thousand starving people with five loaves of bread and two fishes, the resurrection of Lazarus and the son of a widow of Nain—were all demonstrations of the power of His Kingdom of God. Jesus's epic miracle of human creation was another such miracle. The ultimate power of the Spirit of the Father in the human soul of Christ—Jesus's own Kingdom of God—that Jesus used to execute His ultimate miracle provided the evidence for the existence of a living God. Jesus enthroned that His Father as the only true God who reigns and controls all things. The miracle enthroned Jesus as the only one who could reveal His Father. The miracle also revealed Jesus as an authority on the nature of His Father and the nature of all mankind: who we are, why we are here and where we are going. Jesus knows everything about us. We cannot hide from Him. If you think you can hide from Him, ask Paul to recount his experience with the Spirit of the risen Christ on his way to Damascus. Jesus, by using Himself as a model in this miracle, provided the evidence of His divine authority, His power in resurrection, the infinite power of His Kingdom of God and His creative ability.

Jesus's everlasting miracle of the three earthly stages of human creation illuminated the ultimate power of His Kingdom in the human soul, and its irrefutable harmony with it for those who experience it. Jesus's resurrection and the gift of His glorified Holy Spirit that came on the day of Pentecost, prepares the human soul for its transcendental transformation to a new spiritual body in preparation for the divine trinity with the Spirit of Christ and His Father. "That they all may be one; as thou, Father art in me, and I in Thee, that they also may be one in us, that the world may believe that Thou hast sent me." (John 17:21) That was part of Jesus's prayer to His Father for the apostles and for all who believe I Him. In fact, as revealed in the same prayer, it is what awaits all mankind: fellowship with the apostles, Jesus Christ, His Father and with one another. This is the divine trinity of the human souls.

Jesus's epic miracle of human creation, when explored with the periscope of His Kingdom of God, gives mankind not only an insight to the intrinsic value of human life, but also a glimpse into the invisible elements of that kingdom of God. It shows that we can grab it and with it race to our target (the divine trinity of the human souls) as Christ did as a result of that miracle. The miracle is the ultimate proof of the immense power of the Kingdom of God within human souls. It is the power that initiates the earthly phase of human creation, propels and sustains the creative process to its glorious end. We could forget about the Kingdom of God within us and Jesus's miracle and go on killing one another, conducting our daily actions in anger, fear and anxiety about our future. We could continue to live with weapons, hypocrisy, hatred, injustice, illusions of earthly treasures, and a false sense of superiority and control. But we are represented in Christ's ultimate miracle. All aspects of human life are reflected in that miracle. We are active participants in that miracle. That miracle is the reason that the Father sent Jesus down as a human being. Instead of advancing evil in the world, we can use the vital information hidden within the epic miracle to promote world peace, tolerance forgiveness, demonstrate mercy, and show love—love that extends to the enemy, love for the Father, and love Jesus Christ, who sacrificed Himself in order to complete that miracle. My best advice is this: trust in Christ and His Father, obey their commandments, dream of Jesus's Kingdom of God, win it, participate in your own creation and enjoy!

Even as I was writing my last book, *The Father's Business and the Spiritual Cross,* I was sure that the cross was still holding back many of its mysteries. At that time, I did not know some of the things that I am presenting here in this treatise. Like all Christians, I believe in the Easter Faith, handed down to us by Paul as was delivered to him by the early Disciples of Christ. But that robe of Easter Faith is an incomplete garment. When the knowledge of Jesus's Kingdom of God is used as a lens to look at the spiritual events at Golgotha, where Jesus was crucified, the cross yielded up many of its long-buried secrets: Jesus's passwords to the everlasting miracle of human creation that enhanced the comprehension of it, His role in human creation, the role the cross played in protecting mankind from the God of Moses and the Greco-Roman Gods, the nature of His Father, Christ's own nature, the destiny of mankind, the ultimate power of the Kingdom of God and the true meaning of Easter. These are the deep mysteries of the cross. Many of these mysteries were clarified in the epic miracle of life. I must confess that there are still deeper mysteries of the cross that are yet beyond our power to comprehend. However, for now, Jesus enhanced our understanding of His words and works by His demonstration of the epic miracle of human creation. It is important that you contemplate and master every aspect of it. Your future depends on it. Your participation in it and the creation of your own self, as revealed in that three-staged miracle depends on your clear understanding of every aspect of it. It is real. What is amazing is the depth of love bestowed on us by Jesus and the Father in granting us the privilege to participate actively in our own creation. What an honor! All the earthly treasure cannot purchase what is in us already: Jesus's Kingdom of God, preparing and directing the soul, if it is willing, to participate in the creation of a new spiritual creature, bound for the infinite trinity with Christ and His Father. What would you give in exchange for this honor?

What shall it profit a man if he gains the whole world and loses his soul?

---Jesus

In other words, Jesus asks: of what value are all the earthly treasures to a man who spent all his life to acquire them and did not participate in creating himself as demonstrated by Christ's miracle of human creation? The Egyptians buried their Pharaohs with all the precious treasures from their palaces with the conviction that they would use them in afterlife. Today, those treasures are still in the tombs and mankind is slowly taking them away.

The veil that hid the miracle of human creation and the true meaning of Easter was lifted when I recovered the true meaning of Jesus's Kingdom of God and the power it carries along with it. It was the password that unlocked the mystery of Easter and all the three stages of Jesus's everlasting miracle of human creation. The resurrection of Jesus was an event that revealed the result of the glorious earthly end of Jesus's everlasting miracle of human creation as was exhibited by the image of the risen Christ that also showcased the prototype of the new created spiritual human spirit. It was an event that in the final scene of that miracle, revealed the ultimate power of the kingdom of God that came also on the day of Pentecost. It manifested the infinite glory of that Kingdom that came and is within us and provided us with true knowledge of Easter. My dear readers, follow Christ, observe, learn, relax and enjoy His new revelations! Share this vital information with your friends and the leaders of your Christian community. It is amazing.

CHAPTER 1

INITIATION OF JESUS'S EVERLASTING MIRACLE OF THE EARTHLY STAGES OF HUMAN CREATION

*And Jesus went about all Galilee, teaching in their syna-
gogues, and preaching the gospel of the kingdom, and healing all manner of sickness and all manner of disease among
the people. And his fame went throughout all Syria: and they
brought unto him all sick people that were taken with divers
diseases and torments, and those which were possessed with
devils, and those which were lunatic, and those that had the
palsy; and he healed them. And there followed him great multitudes of people from Galilee, and from Decapolis, and from
Jerusalem, and from Judaea, and from beyond Jordan.*

—Matthew 4:23-25

*Go your way, and tell John what things ye have seen and
heard; how that the blind see, the lame walk, the lepers are
cleansed, the deaf hear, the dead are raised; to the poor the
gospel is preached.*

—Like 7:22

Although Jesus's ultimate miracle of human creation is hidden from us, the *modus operandi* that Jesus used are well documented in the Gospel. The activities in the first stage of the miracle—Act 1—are portrayed in the following scenes:

Scene 1 Proclamation of the Kingdom of God
Scene 2 Manifesting the Power of the Kingdom by Performing Miracles
Scene 3 His Discourses on the Parables of the Kingdom of God
Scene 4 Preaching the Sermons and the Beatitudes
Scene 5 Ordination of the Apostles and their First Mission
Scene 6 Jesus's Encounter with Nicodemus

Scene 1-4

Jesus traversed many cities and villages in Palestine performing miracles and preaching about the Kingdom of God. In doing so, Jesus was preparing the soil to plant the seeds of Act 1 of the everlasting miracle of the earthly stages of human creation. He used miracles to promote and launch His Kingdom of God, capturing the attention of the public for what He would ultimately mount as the greatest show on earth. Jesus could pass a sick man on the road and cure him of disease without uttering a single word. Jesus could perform miracles in absentia as was reported when He healed the nobleman's son at the point of death (John 4:46-54) and the Centurion's servant (Luke 7:1-10). Jesus made these miracles a public show for a reason. People were amazed, wondering where Jesus got such power that even the wind and the sea obeyed Him. His popularity surged. Jesus got what He wanted. Great multitudes came together to hear His preaching and to be healed by Him. At one stage, the people wanted to make Him a King. But Jesus quietly withdrew Himself, rejecting that idea. Jesus was not using those miracles to prove His Deity or that He is the expected Messiah. It was not to convince people that He came from God, His Father. Indeed, Jesus was demonstrating the power of the Kingdom of God. However, what nobody understood it at the time is this: He was publicly foreshadowing a bigger miracle yet to come that will reveal Himself and His Father.

From their headquarters in Capernaum, in Galilee, Jesus continued to disseminate information on His Kingdom of God. Again and again, Jesus kept telling people to follow Him. His reason was simple: by following Him, people could learn more about the kingdom of God and participate in the miracle of human creation. Jesus's Kingdom of God was the core element in this miracle of life, its power manifested in all Jesus's miracles. Jesus was also secretly promoting the planned epic miracle. Even as of today, those recorded miracles still promote popular interest in the person and works of Jesus Christ. What Jesus had to do, how He would do it, and how all the stages of the earthly phase of human creation would end, was very clear to Him. Along the way during His mission, Jesus used parables, miracles, sermons, and many other utterances to point to it—but no one comprehended it.

Scene 5
Ordination of the Apostles and their first mission

They are not of the world, just as I am not of the world. Jesus.

---John 17:16

Jesus selected the twelve apostles to participate in His mission. There was no campaign, no referral, no consultation, no election or vote. It was done by deliberate, pre-ordained appointment. By express divine summons of the Father, those twelve eminent servants of God, the Father of Christ, were chosen. The twelve apostles, who were not of this world, were sent to help the Son of Man accomplish the divine mission assigned by the Father. It was a holy assignment by express command of the Father. Jesus said that His Father gave the apostles to Him. Jesus had said that "no man can come unto me, except it were given unto him of my Father." (John 6:65) Jesus trained them work with Him and to publicize the good news of His Kingdom of God to all parts of the world. Their names are in many places in the Gospel. However, it gives me joy to list their names here in this treatise.

Judas (Iscariot), son of Simon.
Simon (Peter) son of Jonas,
Andrew, the brother of Simon,
James, the son of Zebedee,
John, brother of James, son of Zebedee
Philip,
(Bartholomew) Nathaniel,
Matthew (Levi), the son of Alpheus
Thomas (Didymus),
James, the son of Alpheus,
Simon (Zelotes)
Thaddeus (Lebbaeus) also called Judas or Jude, the son of James,

Jesus ordained the twelve apostles. But what is the meaning of this ordination? By their ordination, they were endowed with the Spirit of Truth—the Spirit of the Father through Him. By that ordination, His Spirit will dwell in them, reveal Himself to them, and be part of them. By showering them with His own Spirit, they became a part of Him, too. In essence, this ordination was a practical demonstration of spiritualization of human souls with the Father's Spirit. Only Christ has the power to ordain. It was a demonstration of a significant scene in Act 1 of His planned miracle of human creation.

*Even the Spirit of truth; whom the world cannot receive, because it
sees him not, neither knoweth him: but ye know him; for he dwells
with you, and shall be in you.*

---Jesus said to the apostles. John 14:17

With the men Jesus selected, His mission was successful. Judas
Iscariot, the son of Simon, was one of them. Judas Iscariot was the
only apostle who played an active role in that epic miracle of human creation. If Hollywood were to make a movie of Jesus' miracle
of human creation, only Judas Iscariot from among all the apostles, would receive an Oscar for his supporting role.

The Mission of the Ordained Ambassadors
Without any preamble—again, only Jesus knew what He was doing—He called His twelve disciples together and gave them authority over all devils and the power to cure diseases: "preach,
saying, the kingdom of God is at hand. Heal the sick, cleanse the
lepers, raise the dead, cast out devils; freely you have received,
freely give... Provide neither gold, nor silver, nor brass in your
purses, nor script for your journey, two coats, neither shoes, nor
yet staves: for the worker is worthy of his meat. Whatever house
you enter, stay there until you leave that town. If people do not wel-
come you, shake the dust off your feet when you leave their town,
as a testimony against them." (Matthew 10:7-14), (Luke 9:3-5) Jesus
had demonstrated the power of Kingdom of God by performing
miracles and by forgiving sins. Likewise, He bestowed upon the
apostles the capability to demonstrate the power of the Kingdom
in the same way. In other words, the apostles were not only instructed to announce the coming of the Kingdom of God but also
to manifest its power.

If I cast out devils by the finger of God, then the Kingdom of God is come to you.

--- *Jesus.* Luke 11:20

Likewise, if, by the power endowed to the twelve, they can cast out devils and heal sickness, then also the Kingdom is come unto the people. Never before in the recorded history of Israel, nor indeed the whole world, had such immense power been transferred from one man to other men. However, this transfer of power—spiritualization of human souls—by verbal command of Christ, was new. Jesus was secretly using also the apostles to demonstrate the first earthly stage involved in the miracle of human creation and no one noticed.

Endowed and energized with the power that came from none other than God through His Son, the apostles were ready. With their Master's full protection and the spiritual gifts, they had everything they needed. The commissioned and ordained apostles left in pairs to carry out the will of their Master. They went to villages and cities preaching the kingdom of God, manifested its power by miracles and illustrated its nature by living the life of Christ. Jesus trained and prepared them, not as mere spectators but as active participants in the miracle of human creation that mankind had yet to witness. They would be agents to disseminate what they observed to the world.

Blessed are your eyes, for they see; and your ears, for they hear. For verily I say unto you, that many prophets and righteous men have desired to see those things which ye see and have not seen them and to hear those things which you hear, and have not heard them.

---Jesus to the Apostles. Matthew 13:16, 17

The big question is this: what is the connection between the Kingdom of God within us and Jesus's miracle of the earthly stages of human creation? As we've established, Jesus used the power of His Father in Him for to execute this miracle, using Himself as a human model. Jesus's objective for us is to use the Spirit of His Father within us, given to us through Him, to achieve the same goal and be participants in the miracle of human creation.

In this Act 1, Jesus educated us on His Kingdom of God, demonstrated how we can get it, and endowed some people with that Spirit of the Father as the means for getting us ready to participate in the earthly phase of our creation with the power of the Kingdom of God within us. Act 1 is a double deck of cards. One deck revealed the power of His kingdom of God. The other deck contains the most important set of cards we can play. That set of cards contains instructions on how to enter into Jesus's Kingdom of God, be spiritualized with His Spirit and participate in our own creation. In ordaining the apostles, Jesus dealt us that second deck of cards. Now, we must play our hand.

Scene 6

Jesus's Encounter with Nicodemus
The story of Nicodemus, who came to Jesus at night, is an essential story of human creation. (John 3:1-12) It opened the door for a new creative element that was deployed in the making of the spiritual mankind. That creative element is the Spirit of God. The story of Nicodemus is vital to our understanding of Jesus's Kingdom of God and His everlasting miracle of the earthly phases of human creation. Hidden behind the story is the Father's promise for mankind that Jesus came to this world to demonstrate. It was a story of heavenly things, an introduction to the epistemology of the spiritualization (incarnation) of human souls. The goal of this spiritualization is eternal life. The means to that goal is Jesus's Kingdom of God.

The story portrays the formulation of the Spirit of Christ in the human soul. It exemplifies how the Kingdom of God prepared the human soul for its journey to full expression as a spiritual being. The recorded full story is as follows.

> *There was a man of the Pharisees, named Nicodemus, a ruler of the Jews. The same came to Jesus by night, and said unto him, Rabbi, we know that thou art a teacher come from God: for no man can do these miracles that thou doest, except God be with him. Jesus answered and said unto him, Verily, verily, I say unto thee, except a man be born again, he cannot see the kingdom of God. Nicodemus said unto him, how can a man be born when he is old? Can he enter the second time into his mother's womb, and be born? Jesus answered, Verily, verily, I say unto thee, except a man be born of water and of the Spirit, he cannot enter into the kingdom of God. That which is born of the flesh is flesh; and that which is born of the Spirit is spirit. Marvel not that I said unto thee, ye must be born again. The wind bloweth where it listeth, and thou hearest the sound thereof, but canst not tell whence it cometh, and whither it goeth: so is every one that is born of the Spirit. Nicodemus answered and said unto him, how can these things be? Jesus answered and said unto him, Art thou a master of Israel, and knowest not these things? Verily, verily, I say unto thee, we speak that we do know, and testify that we have seen; and ye receive not our witness. If I have told you earthly things, and ye believe not, how shall ye believe, if I tell you of heavenly things?*

> ---John 3:1-12

The story was not a product of human imagination. It was a real story. Nicodemus was a real person. As a member of the Sanhedrin, he suggested to the other members of the group that Jesus should be allowed to defend Himself. (John 7:50, 51) It was Nicodemus with his friend—Joseph of Arimathaea—who took down the body of Jesus for burial. Nicodemus brought a mixture of myrrh and aloes weighing about a hundred pounds with which they anointed the body of Jesus for burial. (John 19:38-40)

The night encounter Jesus had with Nicodemus was not incidental. Analytical people claim that they usually use the expression "stepping out of the box" to review and understand new things. I do the opposite. I stepped inside the box and used that opportunity to seek in-depth and fact-based analysis of Jesus's discussion with Nicodemus regarding the Kingdom of God and being born with the Spirit. It provided spiritual insights to Jesus's Kingdom of God, the spiritualization of human souls with the Spirit of the Father, His confidence in His Father, and His Father' love and promise for mankind. However, the most intriguing fact that this meeting revealed is that Jesus's Kingdom of God and the spiritualization of human souls hold the mysteries of human life. This *mysterium tremendum et fascinans* (fearful and fascinating mystery) was a revelation of His authoritative power in eternal life and His role in human creation. The words of Jesus on that night revealed the spiritual element we must all possess as we move on, to attain that spiritual life here on earth and after we have died.

Jesus used that opportunity of His encounter with Nicodemus to introduce a new element in the understanding of human creation: that mankind must be born of water and of Spirit. To be born of water is not to be baptized with water. Jesus never baptized anyone with water. Removal of water baptism would not alter the trajectory of the journey of the human soul. It would, however, remove a major obstacle along the path to authentic life. When Jesus revealed a new paradigm in human creation, water baptism has nothing to do with it.

You cannot be born again if you are not born with the Spirit. To be born with the Spirit of Christ is to enter into His Kingdom of God. To be "born again," as Jesus implies to Nicodemus, can only be applied to those who received the Spirit, then lost it as was portrayed in the parable of the Sower—the seeds that fell by the wayside, on the rocks and among thorns. The good ground that received the seed does not need the re-implantation of the seed. We all have the Spirit of the Father given to us through Christ. What you do with it depend on you, as was illustrated in the same parable of the Sower. (Matthew 13:3-9; Mark 4: 3-9; Luke 8: 5-8)

They that are whole need not a physician, but they that are sick. Jesus.

---Matthew 9: 12

The people who are 'whole' do not need to be born again. The human souls that received Jesus's Spirit are already in His Kingdom, manifesting it with justice, mercy, compassion, forgiveness and love that extended to the enemy, as Christ prescribed and demonstrated throughout His life. The human soul that received the Spirit and subsequently lost it—the sick—needs to be born again with the Spirit of Christ. The people that obeyed Jesus's command to sin no more, as well as the thief crucified on His right hand, are examples of those that were born again. The objectives of the spiritualization of human souls are to bond with the Spirit of Christ, to experience that connection as entry into His Kingdom of God and exemplify the Kingdom with compassion, justice, forgiveness, mercy and love that extends to the enemy. The goal of spiritualization—of being born again—is full participation in all earthly stages of human creation for eternal life.

Nicodemus must have been following Jesus secretly, and heard many of His words and witnessed many of His miracles. He sought knowledge and understanding of the new phenomenon that Jesus preached. Having witnessed the manifestations—the miracles—of Jesus's Kingdom of God, he was sure that Jesus came from God. Still, at the time of their conversation, Nicodemus, a master of Israel in religious matters, could not understand why he must be born again, or even what that meant.

Today, without any explanation, Jesus's words to Nicodemus are still blurred. Just like the Jews walked away from Jesus when He told them that they have to "eat His flesh and drink His blood" as to have eternal life (John 6:53-54), many of us would also walk away if He maintained His silence on spiritual rebirth and the meaning of the Kingdom of God. Many Christians today, the Catholics in particular, believe that the wine and the bread offered during the Eucharist represented the real blood and body of Christ. This is a mythical ideology that originated from the Christianity based on sacraments.

In this new revelation, Jesus credited water as the platform of the first human creation that resulted in the first reproductive birth of all mankind. This was a break from the narrative reported by Moses in the book of Genesis that "the Lord God formed man of the dust of the ground, and breathed into his nostrils the breath of life; and man became a living soul." (Genesis 2:7) If, as reported in the book of Genesis, the Creator breathed life into man, and man became a living soul, then Jesus's kingdom of God would be of no value. Jesus's spiritualization of human souls with the Spirit of His Father would be useless, as the human souls had already been spiritualized. Jesus said, "I am come to send fire on the earth; and what will I, if it be already kindled?" (Luke 12:49) The fire is the Spirit of His Father—'what will I, if it (the human soul) be already spiritualized.'

The creation of mankind is an ongoing process. We could apply the same principle to the creation of the Universe. God did not create the entire Universe all at once. We are always finding new discoveries in the Universe. The Father is still creating them, all brand new. We will see more new galaxies, new planets, and exoplanets, and new planets that are not out there yet, but will be created in future. Creation—physical and spiritual—is an ongoing process. The messages that Jesus revealed to Nicodemus and to the people present at that time:

Some human beings born of flesh—the natural birth—are incapable of spiritual life on

their own and must be endowed with the Spirit of the Father in order to gain full
spiritual expression and eternal life
Those who lost this Spirit must be born again with it through Christ
To be born of that Spirit is to enter into His Kingdom of God
Some human beings are already in the Kingdom of God, manifesting their experience of
it, and need not be born again.
Whomsoever that believes in Jesus Christ and in the Father that sent Him, and have
Jesus's kingdom of God will have everlasting life. (John 6:47)

Jesus, without anyone asking Him, gave vivid illustrations of the power and the manifestations of that Spirit for the sake of our understanding. He compared it to the wind that "bloweth where it listeth, and thou hearest the sound thereof, but canst not tell whence it cometh, and whither it goeth: so is every one that is born of the Spirit." (John 3:8) The wind comes in various forms: as powerful hurricanes, cyclones and tropical typhoons or as a gentle breeze. Anyone that has that Spirit can manifest a power like that of the wind.

Who then was this man Nicodemus, who acted as a catalyst that triggered the revelation of all those new, heavenly ideas? Jesus repeatedly talked of people that the Father had tasked him to protect and resurrect. "Therefore said I unto you, that no man can come unto me, except it were given unto him of my Father." (John 6:65) Jesus came down with a team, the apostles, given to Him by His Father. "My Father, which gave *them* me, is greater than all; and no *man* is able to pluck *them* out of my Father's hand." (John 10:29) For a long time, I thought this team included only the apostles and Paul. The apostles and Paul, selected at different times, were in the inner circle of the team. But Nicodemus was a member of the team, too. Nicodemus, like the apostles was resurrected by Christ: "this is the Father's will which hath sent me, that of all which he hath given me I should lose nothing, but should raise it up again at the last day." (John 6:39)

Why are we not like Nicodemus, who went out at night to seek the truth? He saw the manifestations of the power of Jesus's Kingdom of God and sought understanding of what was happening at that time. He was a ruler, a member of the prestigious Sanhedrin group, yet he humbled himself to seek the truth from a Galilean peasant. Jesus gave him a lot to digest, but Nicodemus found that truth. He was transformed—he was born again in the Spirit. .

Nicodemus may not have understood all that Jesus said. Even now, what mortal can really comprehend all that Jesus said and did? Even in this epistemology, I am presenting the revelation of only the few mysteries that I fished out from the infinite ocean of mysteries. Perhaps, Nicodemus, like the apostles, went about the cities and villages in Palestine and outside Palestine, preaching on Jesus's Kingdom of God, manifesting its power and completed his spiritual journey to its glorious end.

Blessed are they which do hunger and thirst after righteousness; for they shall be filled.

---Jesus. Matthew 5:6

CHAPTER 2

JESUS AND THE SPIRITUALIZATION OF HUMAN SOULS

I am come to send fire on the earth; and what will I, if it be already kindled?

— Luke 12:4)

The Father loveth the Son, and hath given all things into His hand. -

–John 3:35

All human beings could have the Spirit of the Father if we are willing. Jesus has the Spirit of the Father in Him. Jesus accomplished all miracles with the power of the Spirit of the Father in Him- His kingdom of God. Our souls need this spiritualization- the endowment of the Spirit of His Father through Jesus Christ) for us to participate in all the earthly stages of our creation as to achieve eternal life. That was precisely what Jesus tried to reveal to the Jews, but they accused Him of claiming to be a God. Their reason was simple: only a God can spiritualize human soul as to make that soul function and have the same nature as God's Spirit. This is in essence the goal of Jesus's Kingdom of God: the connection of the human soul with the Spirit of His Father through Him. That spiritual connection is spiritualization of human soul. It is one of the top secrets Jesus learned from the Father.

> *Then answered Jesus and said unto them, Verily, verily, I say unto you, The Son can do nothing of himself, but what he seeth the Father do: for what things soever he doeth, these also doeth the Son likewise.*

> ---John 5:17

The first time Jesus told the Jews that "the Father is in me and I in the Father," they tried to seize Him, but He escaped. The Jews did not believe that Jesus is the Mediator of the Spirit of God to human souls. It never happened before that a human being was able to do such a thing. Moses and their prophets did not reveal that to them. However, it was one of those things hidden from the wise men, Moses and the prophets. Today, because we have so many different diversified nations and people of different religions and cultures, it would seem something impossible that Jesus is at the center of the endowment of the Spirit of the Father to all human souls. However, on many occasions, Jesus claimed the authority to spiritualize human souls with His Spirit-the Spirit of His Father in Him and demonstrated that by the ordination of His apostles and conferring it to others who manifested the power of the Kingdom that came.

Jesus's role in the spiritualization of human souls was best illustrated in the parable of the Sower.

> *A Sower went out to sow his seed: and as he sowed, some fell by the way side; and it was trodden down, and the fowls of the air devoured it. And some fell upon a rock; and as soon as it was sprung up, it withered away, because it lacked moisture. And some fell among thorns; and*

the thorns sprang up with it, and choked it. And other fell on good ground, and sprang up, and bear fruit a hundredfold. And when he had said these things, he cried, He that hath ears to hear let him hear.

Jesus's disciples asked him, saying, what might this parable be?

And he said, *unto you it is given to know the mysteries of the kingdom of God: but to others in parables; that seeing they might not see, and hearing they might not understand. Now the parable is this: The seed is the word of God. Those by the way side are they that hear; then cometh the devil, and take away the word out of their hearts, lest they should believe and be saved. They on the rock are they, which, when they hear, receive the word with joy; and these have no root, which for a while believe, and in time of temptation fall away. And that which fell among thorns are they, which, when they have heard, go forth, and are choked with cares and riches and pleasures of this life, and bring no fruit to perfection. But that on the good ground are they, which in an honest and good heart, having heard the word, keep it, and bring forth fruit with patience.*

--Luke 8: 5-15

The Sower is Jesus Christ. The ground is the human souls. The seed is the Spirit of the Father in Christ. The Son of man from heaven came down to share that Spirit of the Father in Him-Christ's Spirit-with not only the apostles but all mankind in all nations for a definitive purpose: creation. His apostles and others got that His Spirit and they were able to perform miracles and moved along the path of creative trajectory to their glory. The prolog that Jesus would bestow His Spirit to human souls was first revealed by John the Baptist. "I indeed baptize you with water unto repentance. But he that cometh after me is mightier than

I, whose shoes I am not worthy to bear: he shall baptize you with the Holy Ghost, and with fire."

(Matthew 3:11)

The most important thing Jesus did with the Spirit of the Father in Him-Christ's Spirit-for humankind was to give it as a gift to all who are willing to receive it. Again, that was illuminated by the mission of the seventy disciples. (Luke 10:1-20) When the seventy returned, they said to Jesus:

"Lord, even the devils are subject unto us through thy name."

Jesus said unto them:

"Behold, I give unto you power to tread on serpents and scorpions, and over all the power of the enemy; and nothing shall by any means hurt you. Notwithstanding in this rejoice not, that the spirits are subject unto you; but rather rejoice, because your names are written in heaven."

By bequeathing the Spirit of His Father to us-the spiritualization of human souls-mankind, for the first time, gained the knowledge that if we are willing, we can use it and embark on the journey of preparing ourselves to gain full expression in the imagery of the Father and Jesus Christ, manifesting its glory and power. The earthly evolution of human creation, took a quantum leap from being born again with His Spirit, passed through death-the transitory zone where earthly human beings and human divine activities merge together-to the infinite trinity with the Father and Jesus Christ. The earthly stages of that creative evolutionary process was demonstrated by Jesus's miracle of human creation, enacted through His death and resurrection and powered by His Kingdom of God. Jesus used Himself as a model with the Spirit of His Father in His human soul. Jesus gave us the assurance that we can go through the same creative process with the Spirit of His Father in us through Him-Jesus's Kingdom of God in action within our souls. Spiritualization of human souls and Jesus's Kingdom of God are inseparable and are united in indisputable harmony as demonstrated in Jesus's miracle of human creation. Jesus told Nicodemus that "unless a man is born of the Spirit, he cannot enter into the Kingdom of God." Spiritualization with the Spirit of the Father through Christ is still going on today. It is an invisible process in the creative journey of the soul to its full expression as a new spiritual creature. This human creative trajectory was not for the Jews only or for Christians, but for all mankind in all nations.

The evolutionary earthly stages of human creation, was powered by Jesus's Kingdom of God-the Spirit of the Father through Jesus Christ in human souls. Jesus Christ, the Son of God came down to demonstrate and lead the works of God's plan for human creation to its fulfillment. This is the hidden mystery in the Gospel of John. The human mind was unable to understand what was happening before them at that time.

For God so loved the world, that he gave his only begotten Son, that whosoever believeth in him should not perish, but have everlasting life.

---John 3: 16

But whosoever drinketh of the water that I shall give him shall never thirst; but the water that I shall give him shall be in him a well of water springing up into everlasting life.

---John 4: 14

God, the Father of Jesus can directly give His Holy Spirit to us.

If ye then, being evil, know how to give good gifts unto your children: how much more shall your heavenly Father give the Holy Spirit to them that ask him?

---Luke 11:13

Jesus and His Father have the power to spiritualize, save, protect and resurrect human souls. Even today, Jesus's task in the spiritualization of human souls with the Spirit of His Father in Him is unintelligible because Jesus's kingdom of God, the petitions in the Lord's Prayer for the Kingdom to come and for the Father to give our daily bread, His death, and resurrection are not properly understood. When fully comprehended, we will find ourselves in Jesus's miracle of human creation as we actively participate in the earthly stages of our own creation. We will find Jesus in us and His world in our world. That was the Good News to Paul who found. "Christ in me" and "I in Christ." The Good News to all mankind is the same: that the journey to the eternal life is the journey of creation-the spiritual journey of the human soul as it progresses with the yoke of Christ through death, and resurrection. It is the journey that starts here on Earth and is sustained and directed by Jesus's Kingdom of God within you. To initiate and complete the journey, you must, if you are willing, activate that spiritual bond within us, experience and manifest it. What are you waiting for? *"Take my yoke on."* (Jesus) It is an invitation to take on His Holy Spirit and have a taste of His Kingdom of God.

The importance of this human life pilgrimage as a creative concept is the new platform of creation that was initiated with Jesus's Kingdom of God and demonstrated it in all its three earthly stages, in the everlasting miracle of human creation. This journey of the human soul is not like the pilgrimage of the Jewish people through Egypt to the land of Canaan. It is not the journey of the migrant refugees displaced from their homelands because of war and ethnic conflicts. It is not a journey of people from poor nations seeking better lives in developed nations. It is a spiritual journey of the human soul in its quest to be fully created. It is a journey with the Spirit of Christ as a new companion. It is the journey of all with "Christ in me" acting like little children, sitting in the marketplace, calling unto their fellows to join them, and saying: "We have piped unto you, and ye have not danced; we have mourned unto you, and ye have not lamented." (Matthew 11: 16-17) In essence, the people who understood what was going on invited their friends and family, many of them declined. For Paul, "It is a journey for the high prize of the high calling of God in Christ." (Philippians 3:13-14 It is the journey of the triumphant soul with the spirit of Christ—having survived all life obstacles, both visible and invisible—marching through the pathways lined by angelic hosts and people from all nations that already passed through the path of life, welcoming the newly created Spirit and glorifying the Father and Jesus Christ. It is the journey for the highest prized glory for the human soul. It is a journey powered by Jesus's Kingdom of God. This journey, orchestrated by the Father, set in motion by Christ, is a continuous process, irrepressible and still going on even at this moment. You need the Spirit of Christ for your next spiritual birth that was revealed as the final stage of the epic miracle of human creation, made manifest by His resurrection. Do not leave this planet without it!

For us in this 21st century, the multi-trillion question is this: is the spiritualization of human souls still going on today? If so, is it still being powered by Jesus's kingdom of God? Spiritualization of the human souls is part of the human creative process. How Jesus dispensed this His Spirit, still doing so even of today, is an inscrutable mystery. But there are proofs that it is a continuous irrepressible process powered by Jesus's kingdom of God and that it is still going on even at this moment. First, we still all die. Death is a grand station on the path of all human creative trajectories as demonstrated by Christ in the epic miracle of human creation. It is boundary where the earthly phase of eternal life transcends and transition itself through resurrection to everlasting authentic life. Death is the evidence that the earthly stages of human creation is still going on. Nothing can impede that evolutionary process until the end of time as determined by the Father.

Second, we do not know how Jesus got the Spirit of His Father. The Roman Catholic Church introduced the concept of Immaculate Conception as the answer. Others pointed to His baptism as the time He received it from His Father. The naked truth is that nobody knows. Jesus did not disclose how and when He got it. All we know is that Jesus used that Spirit of His Father in Him to execute all His works, including His epic miracle of the human creation.

Third, Jesus claimed not only the authority as the mediator and dispenser of this Spirit of God to mankind, but also the authority to judge and decide, under the directorship of the Father who gets it. In sending out the twelve apostles on their first unsupervised mission to go out and preach that the Kingdom of God was at hand, Jesus gave them the power to perform miracles. Jesus claimed He has the authority to dispense the Spirit of God in Him to whomsoever He wanted. "All authority has been given to me in heaven and on earth." (Matthew 28:18) "For as the Father hath life in Himself, so hath He to the Son to have life in Himself. And have given Him authority to execute judgment-*on who gets this life through Him*-also, because He is the Son of man." (John 5:25-26) "I say unto you whatsoever ye shall ask the Father-you may ask for His Spirit-in my name, He will give it to you." (John 16:23)

Fourth, the ordination of the apostles and the spiritualization of the souls of the seventy men He sent out on a mission, with the Spirit of His Father, was an authentic proof that human beings can be endowed with His Kingdom of God as they manifested its power. Jesus wants to spiritualize all human souls with the Spirit of His Father. The reason is simple: it has something to do with

Jesus's Kingdom of God and the earthly stages of human creation. This vital information is what is hidden from many prophets and even from righteous men before Jesus came to the world.

> *I am the vine, ye are the branches: He that abideth in me, and I in him, the same bringeth forth much fruit: for without me ye can do nothing. If a man abides not in me, he is cast forth as a branch, and is withered; and men gather them, and cast them into the fire, and they are burned.*

---Jesus. John 15:5-6

It is not possible for all mankind to comprehend this fact now. The reason is simple: many religious leaders, including the current Christianity as it is proclaimed and practiced, have used the current level of human intelligence to deceive mankind. They have used our ignorance not only to enrich themselves but to enthrone themselves as guardians of the truth revealed by Christ. The television Evangelists, the Pentecostal faith healers and the Faith healers who use holy water to cure all diseases used this lack of our knowledge of Jesus's epic miracle of earthly stages of human creation to exploit people and enrich themselves. As we evolve and advance in our intelligence, mankind will see the light of that fact and feel the vibrations of the truth that Jesus revealed. It may take some time to accomplish. Along the path to the revelation of this truth, "Every plant, which my heavenly Father hath not planted, shall be rooted up." (Matthew 15:13)

Again, how did Jesus dispense the Spirit of God to the Apostles? Or did they get it directly from God? The report that "Jesus gave them the power against unclean spirits, to cast them out and to heal all manners of disease." suggests that Jesus dispensed that Spirit of God to them directly. It was already freely given to them by their Master. "Even the Spirit of the truth; whom the world cannot receive, because it seeth him not; neither knoweth him; but ye know him; for he dwelleth with you, and shall be in you." (John 14:17) The Spirit of Jesus Christ that He got from the Farther was already in the apostles. We do not know how Jesus gave the Spirit of His Father to the apostles, and to the seventy men he sent out to preach the Kingdom of God and heal sick people. What we do know is that all of them manifested Jesus's Kingdom of God and their experience of it by the epitome of their lives as exemplified by the life of Christ.

Fifth, after Jesus's ascension, the apostles were again spiritualized by the glorified Spirit of the risen Christ on the day of the Pentecost. The apostles, who experienced it, manifested its power as witnessed by the people in Jerusalem at that time. One can say with confidence that Paul, on his way to Damascus, received it too. After that experience, Paul manifested the power of Jesus's Kingdom of God. What Paul did in the Greco-Roman Empire and the examples of His life after that experience, all pointed the experience of one who was salted with Jesus's Kingdom of God. In essence, Paul entered into Jesus's kingdom of God, achieved its objectives and by his works; Jesus's Kingdom of God grew and expanded beyond our imagination. In these classic examples, their souls were spiritualized with the glorified Spirit of the risen Christ.

The objectives of spiritualization are being manifested today by people all over the world. Its goal is eternal life and knowledge of the Father who sent Jesus Christ. The Christians have not taken the lead in these manifestations. It is very important to outline a brief post-resurrection encounter of Jesus with Peter as a guide in the exploration of the manifestations of spiritualization in the world today. It occurred at the shore of the sea of Tiberius.

So when they had dined, Jesus said to Simon Peter, Simon, son of Jonas, do you love me more than these? He said unto him, Yea, Lord; you know that I love thee. He said unto him, Feed my lambs. He saith to him again the second time, Simon, son of Jonas, do you love me? He said unto him, Yea, Lord; you know that I love thee. He said unto him, Feed my sheep. He said unto him the third time, Simon, son of Jonas, do you thou me? Peter was grieved because he said unto him the third time, do you love me? And he said unto him, Lord, you know all things; you know that I love thee. Jesus said unto him, Feed my sheep.

---John 21:15-17

Peter and the other apostles carried out that instruction by setting up the first non-gated Christian community. Paul collected money from the disciples in the Greco-Roman Empire to support them in the care of the poor. They went to many cities and villages preaching the gospel of the Kingdom of God and the news of the resurrection of Christ. Today, the instruction to 'feed my sheep' is still being carried out. Today, one such example of the sheep is the migrant refugees. What the German Chancellor and the German people that supported her did for those refugees revealed the irrepressible working infrastructure in Jesus's Kingdom of God in people who have entered into it. They are manifesting it with compassion, love, mercy justice and forgiveness. How they got it is still hidden. As I was writing this epiphany, it was reported that Nigeria Defense Headquarters established a camp to rehabilitate and integrate members of repentant Boko Haram group. What they have demonstrated, on what they described as Operation Safe Corridor under the leadership of President Muhammadu Buhari, is forgiveness and love that extended to the enemy that was consistent with what Christ prescribed and demonstrated. Today, many people are feeding the sheep. To feed the sheep is to love Christ and the Father that sent Him. To love Christ and His Father is to enter into Jesus's kingdom of God. To enter into that Kingdom is to be spiritualized with the Spirit of His Father through Christ and be a participant in the epic miracle of human creation that is still going on now as was demonstrated by Christ. This miracle, like all other Jesus's miracles was propelled by the power of His Kingdom.

Jesus's sheep presented in many forms during His mission. He was a friend to the sinners, the wine nibblers, the sick people, the poor and the children. They were His sheep. Jesus insisted that if we feed them and gives them even a cup of cold water in His name, that you have loved Him. Jesus said that "If a man loves me, he will keep my words: and my Father will love him, and we will come unto him, and make our abode with him." (John 14:23) To accept that invitation, is to receive the Spirit of His Father and enter into Jesus's Kingdom of God. This is the passport to eternal life. It is happening today. In this 21st century as it was in the past, Jesus's sheep are the poor, victims of drug abuse, alcoholics, the homeless, the sick, people subjected to racism, people subjected to economic slavery by the people who govern them, people subjected to poverty by nation who exploit them by siphoning off their natural resources, the refugees who are victims of war and the neglected children. If you love Jesus and His Father, then feed His sheep as you enter into His Kingdom of God and be propelled along the human trajectory by the power of that Kingdom.

> *Not everyone that saith unto me, Lord, Lord, shall enter into the kingdom of heaven; but he that doeth the will of my Father which is in heaven. Many will say to me in that day, Lord, Lord, have we not prophesied in thy name? And in thy name have cast out devils? And in thy name done many wonderful works? And then will I profess unto them, I never knew you: depart from me, ye that work iniquity.*

---Jesus. Matthew 7:21-23

We are a blessed generation. What Jesus accomplished, as it unfolds, will lead mankind to unprecedented global spiritualization. It will continue to manifest in human souls. In its irrepressible growth, it will advance and sustain this gift of the Father to human souls. During this era of prodigious spiritualization of human souls, many souls will advance to full expression in the spiritual image as new creatures. Today, it would seem that world religions exist to fight one another and this animosity is even experienced within the same group. With this vital information on the spiritualization of human souls and the revealed knowledge of Jesus's Kingdom of God and what would be revealed in Jesus's epic miracle of human creation, it is my hope that ultimately the religious divisions among many communities and nations would one day vanish and the world will be at peace. We will all die one day. Start the preparation now, that when it happens, you have made all preparations and equipped yourself for the performance of your own miracle of creating yourself with the power of Jesus's Kingdom of God: to die with the implanted Spirit of Christ!

Fear not, little flock; for it is your Father's pleasure to give you the Kingdom.

---Luke 12:32

What? Know ye not that your body is the temple of the Holy Ghost (the glorified Spirit of the risen Christ) *which is in you, which ye have of God, and ye are not your own?*

Paul 1 Corinthians 6:19

CHAPTER 3

THE DIRECTOR OF THE MIRACLE: GOD, THE FATHER OF JESUS CHRIST

Believest thou not that I am in the Father, and the Father in me? The words that I speak unto you I speak not of myself: but the Father that dwelleth in me, He doeth the works.

—John 14:10

If the reality of God is an important issue in human creation and life, the question of who is the Creator and who we worship should be given a propitious priority. Perhaps, at this stage in the exploration of Jesus's everlasting miracle of the earthly stages of human creation, we have to examine the God who planned and controlled it. The Jewish God was revealed in the book of Genesis by Moses as the Creator of mankind. Jesus presented His Father as the only true God who reigns and controls human life. In this battle of the two Gods, the God of Moses and God, the Father of Jesus, on who is the Creator, the winner will be the God, who will give a practical demonstration of a phase in the creative process. That was precisely what Jesus did for His Father in His everlasting miracle of the earthly stages of human creation.

To this end was I born, and for this cause came I unto the world.

---Jesus

The God whom Jesus called His Father is not the God that Moses revealed to the Jews.

The Father Himself, which hath sent me, hath borne witness of me.
Ye have neither heard His voice at any time, nor seen His shape.

---John 5:37

Who is this His Father? However, Jesus said, "I know Him, for I am from Him, and He hath sent me." (John 7:29) The God Moses revealed to the Jews, came down on Mount Sinai and by direct speech, delivered the Ten Commandments to Moses. (Exodus 20: 3-17; Deuteronomy 5: 6-21) The same God spoke to Moses and other people on many occasions. It was reported in the Old Testament literature that on Mount Sinai, He gave to Moses "two tablets of stones written with finger of God." (Exodus 31:18) From what Jesus said, before He came to the world, no one saw the shape of His Father or heard His voice. Who was the God that spoke to Moses and revealed Himself to him? Jesus is not the Son of that Jewish God.

God, the Father of Jesus Christ, sent Him to the world to give an enduring proof of what Himself and Jesus Christ has been doing for mankind: creating us. Jesus used Himself as a model in the performance of the epic miracle of human creation, controlled by His Father, and gave the strongest evidence that His Father is the Creator and that He is also a creator. The God of Moses played no role in Jesus's miracle of human creation.

It would seem that God, the Father of designed the cross. The Father did not design the cross. Jesus and His Father had waited for centuries for the time to be fulfilled for what happened in Jerusalem. They watched us from their spiritual world. They watched as we kill one another and as one nation attacked the other to take their treasuries and carry off their women and children. They watched the good and the evil activities of mankind. They sent wise people to guide us. Some of them were killed. Jesus did not come to Palestine when the Babylonians or the Assyrians occupied it. Patience became the virtuous *modus operandi* deployed for what they wanted to accomplish. The Romans were not the first to use crucifixion, but they popularize it. The Father did not order the crucifixion of Jesus. Even before Emperor Augustus was born, Jesus and His Father knew what the Romans would do. They had waited for that opportunity. They took advantage of it and allowed it to happen.

Who is this Father, who used the abominable infamous stake-the cross that the Romans used to crucify the Jews-to accomplish His holy purposes? Of all the weapons at His disposal-legions of angelic forces, His power-His Father chose the shameful *modus operandi* of crucifixion for Jesus. Crucifixion of the Jews on the cross by the Romans, was considered to be the most inhumane and loathsome act ever perpetuated by nations that had conquered them. By handing Him over to the Romans to be crucified, the Jewish authorities wanted to bring shame upon Jesus and humiliate Him. Jesus accepted it because He had the knowledge that His Father designed it. Jesus, with His omniscient attributes from His Father, knew the benefits of His action.

Ye neither know me, nor my Father; if ye had known me, ye should have known my Father also.

---John 8:19

The works which the Father hath given me to finish, the same works that I do, bear witness of me, that the Father hath sent me. And the Father himself, which hath sent me, hath borne witness of me. Ye have neither heard his voice at any time, nor seen his shape.

---John 5:36-37

I am not come of myself, but He that sent me is true, whom ye know not.

---John 7:28

All things are delivered to me of my Father: and no man knoweth who the Son is, but the Father; and who the Father is, but the Son, and he to whom the Son will reveal him.

---*Luke 10:22*

The Father that people never heard of was revealed to the world by Jesus. In the Temple, Jesus told the Jews: "Ye neither know me nor my Father. If ye had known me, ye should have known my Father also." (John 8:19) This new God, Jesus called His Father-that no one ever saw His shape or heard His voice-is not the Jewish God that revealed Himself to Abraham, Moses and others, as recorded in the Old Testament literatures. The God of Moses spoke to the people of Israel through Moses. (Exodus 3:4-14) and the prophets with the proclamations that He is "the only God among you, and there is no God except me." (Isaiah 45:14-15; 45:20-21; Hosea 13:4) The Father of Jesus spoke to mankind through Jesus. (John 8:26; 14:10) Jesus made it clear that His Father is the only true God. (John 17:3) The Gospel of John, the apostle Peter and Paul made many references to the Father of Jesus. The critical question is this: whose voice did Moses and the prophets hear? It was reported in the book of Genesis that God appeared to Abraham. Genesis 17:1) Moses, Aaron, Nadab, Abihu and seventy of the elders of Israel saw the God of Israel including His feet. (Exodus 24:9-10) That was definitely not the God, the Father of Jesus, as no one ever saw His shape.

Jesus was the executor, the principal actor of the everlasting miracle of the earthly phases of human creation. We would like to know who was directing it. Is it the new God that Jesus introduced to the world as His Father or the God who revealed Himself to Moses? This is the reason why I have introduced this epiphany now before moving forward with further exploration of Jesus's epic miracle of life as to reveal the God that directed that miracle. The God of Israel was credited with human creation, as was reported by Moses in the book of Genesis. (Genesis 1:27) There must be something we do not know about this God who created human beings in His own image, then expelled them from that place when His ultimate purpose for them was still unfulfilled. As of today, no one, not even the Jews, has a definitive plan from the God on how we can regain entry into the place where we were first created. The Jews have a plan that calls for the new Paradise-a new Jerusalem-on earth to be established when the promised Messiah would come. They are still waiting for that Messiah.

What Jesus introduced by this miracle of human creation that was showcased by His resurrection, was quite different from the record of creation in the book of Genesis. What Jesus proclaimed and demonstrated by this miracle portrayed that human beings are still been created; that there is an earthly phase of human creation. In His Discussion with Nicodemus, Jesus pointed out that we must be born of water and of spirit for full expression of our creative life. In essence, human life that started with water has to be spiritualized. Perhaps all these creative processes started on this planet and would continue on this planet. This is consistent with what Jesus said that we are from here. This is in sharp contrast with what was recorded by Moses in the book of Genesis that the God

He revealed "formed man-Adam-out of the dust of the ground and breathed into his nostrils the breath of life; and man became a living soul." (Genesis 2:7) And the same God made a woman-Eve-from one of the ribs He took from Adam. (Genesis 2:21-23)

This Jesus's Father gave Him all authorities in heaven and on earth and nobody knows this Father except those to whom He would give that privilege information

All things are delivered to me of my Father: and no man knoweth who the Son is, but the Father; and who the Father is, but the Son, and he to whom the Son will reveal him.

---Luke 10:22

When Jews asked Jesus: "Where is thy Father?" Jesus responded and said, "I know Him, for I am from Him, and He hath sent me." (John 7:29) God, the Father revealed by Jesus is not the God, who in the beginning created the heavens, and all the earth-including Adam and Eve-in six days and rested on the seventh day as was reported by Moses. ((Genesis 1:1-31; 2:2) The six days one time creation brought much confusion to the Father's phased evolutionary process of creation of all living things and the galaxies. This Father revealed two thousand years ago by Jesus, is still creating mankind, new galaxies, new plants and animals. Darwin theory of the origin of species triumphed because of the false concept of six day creation and the gross misconception that Jesus was sent to the world to save the descendants of Adam and Eve-driven out of the Paradise by the God who created them-and to help mankind to prepare for the future Kingdom of God to be established on this planet Earth. The misrepresentation of the death of Jesus Christ as ransom, atonement and sacrifice for sins, enthroned the Darwin theory of creation. The eyewitnesses saw the resurrected Jesus and rejoiced with joy that 'He is risen.' The inability to understand the prototype of what was revealed on Easter drove mankind to the Big Bang theory of creation. The irrepressible plan of that Father for staged creation of mankind and the Universe-as I will reveal in this treatise is running its course on schedule.

Mankind have worshipped many Gods and called Gods by many names. Many of the Gods just simply vanished. The Egyptian Pharaoh Akhenaten, who died in BC 1336, called this God, Aten and built a temple for Him. The Jews have given many names to their God, such as Yahweh, Elohim (God), El Olam (God everlasting), El Elyyon (God, Most High) and El Shaddai (God Almighty). Subsequently, they built a temple at Jerusalem for this God of Abraham, Isaac, Jacob and Moses. Jesus introduced a new God, hidden from humanity since the beginning of time, called this God His Father and refused to assign a name to this His Father. He was not interested in building a temple with human hands for His Father. Many Christians are still confused about this Father, misrepresenting Him as the God of the Jews revealed in the book of Genesis by Moses as a Creator. The ridiculousness of this is that they still believe in the Father of Jesus Christ as the God who created all things. They believe in everything Jesus said about Him. They Jehovah Witnesses, a Christian community who believes in Christ, address the God they worship as Jehovah, the same God that Moses revealed to the Jews. Their Faith is grounded in both the Old and New Testament literature and in the book of Revelations.

If Jesus had revealed more things about the God that created Adam and Eve and illuminated His image, the Jews would have embraced Him as the expected Messiah. If the words and works of Jesus fulfilled all the predictions of their Prophets, they would have hailed Him as the Anointed One of Israel. If Jesus indeed fulfilled the laws in the Torah and in Midrash and enhanced their interpretations, the Jews would have accepted Him as the Son of Man as revealed by the Prophet Daniel. If all the sacred practices for their God-animal sacrifices for atonement of sins, Sabbath day observances and others-were promulgated and observed by Jesus, the Jews would have appointed Him the High Priest and head of the Sanhedrin Council. If all the teachings and miracles of Jesus opened to the Jews, the hope of salvation and the fulfillment of all the covenants with their God, they would not have condemned Jesus to death.

Jesus Christ not only introduced a new God to the Jewish people but was also promoting the worship of that new God and the abandonment of the worship of the Jewish God in the Temple at Jerusalem. Passing through Samaria, Jesus said to the lady that gave Him water; "Woman, believe me, the hour cometh, when ye shall neither in this mountain, nor yet at Jerusalem, worship the Father." (John 4:21) With reference to the Temple at Jerusalem that was made with hands, Jesus told His apostles that it would be destroyed. (Matthew 24:1) Publically He told the Jews that He was going to build another made without hands. (Mark 14:58)

Human life without the spirit is no life at all. The Father that Jesus presented to the Jews is a Spirit with life. The God that the Jews worship also is portrayed as a Spirit with life. The book of Genesis-as reported by Moses-revealed that after the creation of man from the dust of the ground, He breathed into their nostrils the breath of life and man became a living soul. (Genesis 2:7) Jesus said that His "Father hath life in Himself; so hath he given to the Son to have life in himself." (John 5:26) This life is the Spirit of the Father. Metaphorically, Jesus called the Spirit of God in Him the bread of God and claimed the authority to give it to mankind. "For the bread of God is he which cometh down from heaven, and gives life unto the world." (John 6:33) Without reference to the God of creation in the book of Genesis, Jesus claimed that in creation the endowment of spiritual life in humans is by His Father and Himself. Jesus revealed His Father as the Creator God and accredited all phases of human creation and the creation of both the visible and things that are not visible to us now, to His Father, who works every day, even on Sabbath days. Whether God the Father initiated the creation of humans with dust of the ground or with water as revealed by Jesus will be discussed later...

Jesus portrayed His Father as a merciful God: "Be therefore merciful as your Father is also merciful." (Luke 6:36) The God of Moses enthroned the first born of the Jews as His special children. (Exodus 13:1) The same God destroyed the entire first born of the Egyptians including the first born of their beasts. (Exodus 11:1-6)

Jesus introduced a divine Father who sees in secret, rewards secretly and knows everything we do. "But when you give alms, let not your left hand know what your right has done. That your alms may be in secret: and thy Father who sees in secret He shall reward you openly." (Matthew 6:3-4) The reward is not land. The reward was the gift of His Spirit to all mankind through Christ. This gift is for everlasting life. In his encounter with the Samaritan woman, Jesus said unto her, "If you know the gift of God, and who it is that said to you, Give me to drink; thou would have asked of him, and he would have given thee, living water. Whosoever drinks of this water shall thirst again: But whosoever drinks of the water that I shall give him shall never thirst; but the water that I shall give him shall be in him a well of water springing up into everlasting life." (John 4:10, 13-14) The God of Moses rewarded the Jewish people with the 'Promised Land,' in Palestine in accordance with the promise He made to Abraham. "And I will give unto thee and to thy seed after thee, the land wherein thou art a stranger, all the land of Canaan, for an everlasting possession; and I will be their God." (Genesis 17:8)

Jesus characterized His Father as a good God who loves all humankind. Jesus, in all His utterances did not reveal that His father was angry at humanity. The God of Moses got angry and drove away Adam and Eve from existence in the Paradise before His ultimate plan for them was fulfilled. The chosen people for the God of Moses are the Jews. The Father makes the sun to rise on the evil and on the good, and sends rain on the just and on the unjust." (Matthew 5:45) "God is kind even to the unthankful as to the evil." (Luke 6:35) The God of Moses punishes the enemies of Israel. Jesus revealed a God, His Father that forgives the enemy. The finest illustration of the loving, forgiving and the compassionate Father was portrayed in the story of the prodigal son. (Luke 15:11-24)

If I honor myself, my honor is nothing: it is my Father that honored me; of whom ye say, that He is your God: Yet ye have not known Him; but I know Him: and if I should say, I know Him not, I shall be a liar like unto you: but I know Him, and keep His saying.

---John 8:54-55

What I am trying to portray here is not new. The apostles, Paul and other stood up once and proclaimed it. In the second century after the Apostolic Age, Marcion Christianity proclaimed it, and alerted the Christians that the God of Moses is not the same God, the Father that Jesus revealed to the world. Today, Christianity must stand up and proclaim their God! They must proclaim in unequivocal term, in a way that a child would understand it, the God, the Father of Jesus is our God. It is not a historical or theological exercise. Human earthly lives depend on it. The knowledge of Jesus's Kingdom of God and its mysteries depend on it. The knowledge why Jesus, without offering any resistance, allowed Himself to be crucified and died depends on it. The knowledge of why the Father sent Jesus to this world depends on it. The knowledge of what was finished at Golgotha depends on it. The past history of the current Christianity is both good and bad. Many pages of its history-the religious wars-were written with ink of human blood. This is not what God, the Father of Jesus wants. Christianity must stand up today and say to the world; "The God of Moses is not our God." The men and women-the apostles, Mary Magdalene and other women, Paul and other disciples-did that and became free. It is in having done so, that the great glory of the new Christianity, proclaimed by Christ, persists to the present age. It is not too late for us to do the same.

Everything that Jesus did was with the Spirit of His Father and not with the Spirit of the God of Moses. Jesus's kingdom of God is powered by the Spirit of His Father. The Spirit of His Father was involved in all stages of the everlasting miracle of the human creation that was played out as epic events. God, the Father of Jesus, and not the God of Moses, controlled all the events in that miracle. Jesus was the authorized executor of the epic miracle of human creation.

The Father loveth the Son, and hath given all things into His hand.

---John 3: 35

CHAPTER 4

PROVOCATIVE ACTS OF JESUS DIRECTED AGAINST JEWISH AND ROMAN AUTHORITIES

Behold, we go to Jerusalem, and the Son of man shall be delivered unto the Gentiles, and shall be mocked, and spitefully entreated, and spitted on; And they shall scourge Him, and put Him to death, and the third day He shall rise again.

—Luke 18: 31–33

A woman when she is in travail hath sorrow, but because her hour is come, but as soon as she is delivered of the child, she remembered no more the anguish, for the joy that a man is born into the world.

—John 16:21

The initiation of Act 2 of Jesus's miracle of the earthly stages of human creation started with His planned trip to Jerusalem. It ended at Golgotha where He was crucified. Jesus always asked people to follow Him. We must follow Jesus to Jerusalem, to Golgotha and beyond to see the "woman in travail." We must be in the delivery room to witness the birth of a child and participate in the joy that a child has been born into the world. What Jesus was telling everyone is to follow Him to Jerusalem and be a witness to the everlasting miracle of the earthly stages of human creation. Jesus used Himself as the main actor in that miracle. You would think that 'the man' that is born into the world that was showcased on Easter morning is the glorified Spirit of Jesus Christ. It is more than that. The whole mystery of Jesus's everlasting miracle of the earthly phase of human creation is rooted in what His Kingdom of God accomplished. Without the power of that Kingdom of God, the execution of that miracle would not have been possible. If you have activated that Kingdom of God within your human soul, you can be a participant in the miracle of human creation and with its infinite power, "ye might say unto this sycamine tree, Be thou plucked up by the root, and be thou be planted in the sea; and it shall obey you." (Luke 17:6)

Jesus left Bethany with His apostles to reveal one of the deep mysteries of His kingdom of God. By His crucifixion and the death in the performance of the miracle of the earthly phase of human creation, Jesus revealed the infinite power of His Kingdom, His Father, Himself and who we are, but no one took notice. Who could understand what Jesus was doing without deep knowledge why He came to this world? What would happen at Golgotha was kept secret. Jesus resorted to metaphors, parabolic and symbolic expressions, and illustrations to tell the people about the final events of His mission. The images of the woman in travail, the corn of wheat, the cup, the baptism that He must be baptized with, and the lifting up of the Son of man were the metaphoric expressions in the Gospel that Jesus used to demonstrate His death and the glory of it. How can we penetrate into the depths of what Jesus was trying to accomplish? I am sure that knowledge would trigger stupendous evolutionary development in our earthly phase of our creation which will allow us to develop an infinite union with the Father and Jesus Christ

"And they were on the way going up to Jerusalem; and Jesus went before them; and they were amazed; and as they followed, they were afraid."

---Mark 10:32

What was thought to be catastrophic and humiliating events in Jerusalem, spontaneous utterances, unrehearsed parables, innovative miracles, were indeed well organized provocative acts by Jesus, to antagonize the Jewish authorities to take action against Him. Those provocative acts led to His condemnation to death by the Jewish authorities and crucifixion by the Romans. The cross was the indispensible tool Jesus used in the everlasting miracle.

When ye have lifted up the Son of man, then shall ye know that I am He.

---John 8:28

The everlasting miracle of the earthly stages of human creation designed by His Father and executed by Jesus, was the best-kept secret in the history of heavenly and earthly events. What happened during that period will never again be repeated because the miracle achieved all its objectives and goals. The secrecy and the silence maintained by Jesus guaranteed the successful completion of that miracle. It was done to protect the truth that was eventually revealed. It was done to protect Jesus's Kingdom of God. It was done to protect humanity. To have revealed any information on Jesus's modus operandi in the performance of that miracle would have not only endangered the lives of the ordained apostles but that of Jesus Himself before He was lifted up on the cross. If the Jews had known what Jesus was doing and the end result of it, they would not have condemned Him to death.

The completion of the miracle was vital because many things were at stake. The revelation of the Father as the Creator and only true God depended on it. The knowledge of Jesus's spiritualization of the human souls with the Spirit of His Father for the completion of our creation depended on it. The control of obstacles to Jesus's Kingdom of God and to humanity depended on it. The revelation of Jesus as a Creator and also as a God depended on it. The revelation of fully created spiritual beings and the final human glory depended on it. The knowledge of how the Father and Jesus Christ have been creating mankind, even before Jesus come to the world depended on the successful execution of all the three Acts of that everlasting miracle. Our ability to have a glimpse into other spiritual worlds of the Universe depended on it. It was a miracle that opened our understanding of the words and works of Christ. It was a miracle that gave us the platform on which to stand in looking at today's world and all the inhabitants of the world as same humanity. It was a miracle that revealed the deep mysteries of His Kingdom of God. It was a miracle the revealed all the mysteries of Golgotha and why Jesus died. Jesus's epic everlasting miracle of the earthly stages of human creation is the story of His love and that of His Father for mankind.

Greater love hath no man than this, that a man lay down his life for his friends.

---Jesus. John 15:13

Jesus first predicted His death to His apostles at Caesarea Philippi when He told them that He "must go to Jerusalem and suffer many things at the hands of the elders, chief priests, and teachers of the law, and be killed and on the third day be raised." (Matthew 16:21) It was an admission of the secret plan the Father and Himself had worked out before Jesus's earthly birth. Jesus, as was His custom, did not tell them the reason why He had to die or explain why it had to be at Jerusalem or why He had to be lifted up on a cross at Golgotha. During His last days in Jerusalem, Jesus was hastening things up for an event that He did not see as a catastrophe but as what He must do to complete the epic miracle of human creation by using Himself as the model. The tragic, humiliating, scornful events in Jerusalem were God's own directed spiritual events. It is my desire that you too will develop spiritual eyes and be a witness to the everyday heavenly miracle of human creation that was showcased on earth.

As soon as Jesus left Bethany for that last trip to Jerusalem, everything changed. What was reported in the Gospel as jubilant but unproductive events during Jesus's last days in Jerusalem were indeed lamp posts that illuminated His way to the glorious end of the everlasting miracle. To gain insight into the mysteries of the second Act of Jesus's everlasting miracle of earthly stages of human creation, it is important to look at provocative acts of Jesus directed against the Jewish authorities and the Roman Governor Pontius Pilate, before Jesus was crucified at Golgotha. Jesus knew what He was doing. At the end of that second day in Jerusalem, Jesus disclosed the manner of His death: the cross. "You know that after two days is the feast of the Passover, and the Son of man is betrayed to be crucified." (Matthew 26:2) That was sad news to all the apostles who heard Him. That was the first time Jesus used the word "crucified" to describe His own death. "When you shall have lifted up the Son of man, (on the cross) then shall you know that I am He." (John 8:28) Jesus was the only one at that time who talked about His crucifixion. He had to be on that cross. Jesus knew that the Romans will crucify Him. All that happened in Jerusalem had a divine purpose. The Jewish authorities and Pontius Pilate were used for its accomplishment. That divine purpose was to reveal why His Father sent Him to the world through the everlasting miracle of the earthly stages of human creation. Jesus had to use Himself as a model.

As the Father knoweth me, even so know I the Father: and I lay down my life for the sheep.

---John 10:15

Jesus spent three years preaching on the Kingdom of God before His death and continued to do so after His resurrection. Jesus's kingdom of God also holds the key to the revelation of the mysteries of Jesus's last journey to Jerusalem. When the mystery of Jesus's last journey to Jerusalem was revealed, it showed the absolute control the invisible Father had over all the events. Jesus was following every step in God's plan. Jesus knew His final frontier would be at Jerusalem, where He would finish His own assignment.

Scene 1

The Triumphant Entry into Jerusalem

Jesus knew that the chief priest and the Jewish authorities were planning to kill Him in Jerusalem, yet in His last days, He entered Jerusalem like a king returning from a victorious encounter with the enemy. When the crowd heard that Jesus was coming to Jerusalem, "they took branches of palm trees, and went forth to meet him and cried, 'Hosanna to the son of David: Blessed is He that cometh in the name of the Lord; Hosanna in the highest." (Matthew 21:9) The whole crowd cheered and hailed Him as King, the long-awaited Redeemer from the root of King David. The jubilation and the ecstasy of the people were beyond measure. The Hosanna song erupted everywhere as people, including children, spread palm leaves on the road. The Jewish priests noted that "all the Jerusalem is moved" and "that the whole world is gone after Him." They asked Jesus to put an end to the event: "Master, rebuke your disciples." But Jesus replied, "I tell you that, if these should hold their peace, the stones would immediately cry out." (Luke

19:39–40) Who in his or her right mind would not fall for Jesus, who spoke with power as no man had spoken before? Who had performed so many miracles by then that even if another Christ came, would that Christ perform more miracles? Whose wisdom and power was beyond measure. How could you not fall for Him? How could you not revere Him, who raised Lazarus from the dead though he had been dead for three days? How could we not believe He was the Lord of resurrection? The triumphant entry of Jesus into Jerusalem rekindled the Jewish aspiration for the restoration of the glory to Israel, the establishment of the Kingdom of God in Palestine and the expulsion of the Romans. The people were exited and wanted to declare Jesus a King.

A few days before Jesus entered into Jerusalem, the chief priests and the Pharisees, under the directorship of the High Priest Caiaphas, called a council together to plan how to put Jesus to death. An edict, a commandment from the high priest and the Pharisees in authority, was passed and circulated among the people that if anyone knew where Jesus was, he or she had to reveal it so that the authorities could arrest him. "Now both the chief priests and the Pharisees had given a commandment, that, if any man knew where he was, he should show it, that they might take him." (John 11:57) Jesus knew about the edict, yet five days before the Passover, Jesus staged the greatest victory gala as He marched into Jerusalem. What was Jesus's inner motive? Why was He fearless?

The triumphant entry into Jerusalem had a divine purpose. The Jewish and Roman authorities were used for its accomplishment. Jesus's triumphant entry into Jerusalem was not an aspiration or an acceptance of the anticipated Jewish Messianic status. Jesus never said He was the Jewish Messiah. The stylish, royal entry into Jerusalem was not to establish the new kingdom of God with Jerusalem as the headquarters. The Passover crowd and the apostles saw in Him the fulfillment of all the prophetic utterances of the expected Messiah, the Redeemer of Israel. Jesus never said He was a Redeemer of Israel. It was not Jesus's intention to march into Jerusalem and rescue His people from the Romans.

Jesus maintained His silence on the reasoning behind His actions. To penetrate into the deep mystery of what was going on; one must know the objectives and the goals of Jesus's Kingdom of God. The problem is that we have carried the ignorance the meaning of Jesus's Kingdom of God too far, even to the present generation that many things that Jesus said and did became elusive. For this reason, the demonstration of the epic miracle of human creation remained hidden. What is happening in the world today shows that the spiritual evolution of the entire human race is still in its rudimentary phase.

Jesus had to be put on that cross for His miracle of human creation to be accomplished. Jesus was acting according to the outline in the divine plan the Father designed. People that participated had no control over their actions. The invisible God was in control. Human beings participated in the events at Jerusalem and at Golgotha, but they only played the role that was assigned to them. The provocation of the Jewish and Roman authorities was *the modus operandi* Jesus used to get Himself on the cross.

Scene 2

Cleansing of the Temple
On the same day Jesus marched into Jerusalem, He went to the temple and cleansed it. "Jesus went into the temple, began to cast out them that sold and bought in the temple, and overthrew the tables of the money changers and these of them that sold doves. And would not suffer any man should carry any vessels through the temple." (Mark 11:15–16)

Why was Jesus angry at the traders who provided services at the outer court of the temple, where worshippers can exchange their money and buy animals for sacrifices? Such practices started in the days of Abraham and became highly commercializes when the first temple was built. Jesus's parents took Him to the temple on many occasions during the Jewish festivals celebrated in the temple at Jerusalem. I am quite sure that they too bought something in the temple they used for sacrifice. During the last feast of the Tabernacle, Jesus was in the Temple with His brothers and sisters. Again, His siblings must have bought something from the traders that they used for sacrifice. At that time, Jesus saw the traders and the money exchangers and took no action. Why then did Jesus, during the last visit to Jerusalem, went to the temple and cleansed it? By doing so, Jesus touched the very essence of the Jewish religious service. No Jew would stand for it. However, by cleansing the temple, Jesus got what He wanted. The Jewish authorities intensified their plan to kill Jesus when they heard what He did in the temple. "And the scribes and the chief priests heard it; they sought how they might destroy Him." (Mark 11:18) Jesus knew the reason for His provocative act but refused to discuss it with anyone. He knew the part the Father assigned to the Jewish authorities, but their killing Him was not in the plan.

Scene 3

Parables of the Man with Two Sons and the Wicked Husbandmen During this period, most of Jesus's discussions were centered on the Jewish authorities. His speech was no longer a sermon but inflammatory words against the Jewish authorities. What people witnessed was not a humble man who in the past spoke with goodness but Jesus of Nazareth, a man with power and authority directing all actions against the Jewish leaders. The parables of the man with two sons (Matthew 21:28–32) and of the wicked husbandmen (Matthew 21:33–45; Mark 12:1-12; Luke 20:9-19) were directed to the Jewish authorities.

The parable of the two sons depicted the story of two sons who were asked to do something by their father. One of them said he would not do it. Later, he changed his mind and did the work. The other son said that he would do it. However, he failed to do it. The interpretation is perceptible in the parable. The Jews knew that Jesus was talking about them. The son who promised the do the work, but failed to do so, depicted the Jews who promised to obey God's laws and commandments but failed to do so. The son who first refused to do the work, but later changed his mind and did the work represented those whom Jesus portrayed in the parables of the lost (the lost sheep, Matthew 18:12-14, Luke 15:3-7; the lost coin, Luke 15:8-10; the Prodigal son, Luke15:11-32) and the publicans and sinners that ate with Him. Those people believed in His words and repented. They are those who will inherit the kingdom of God.

In the parable of the wicked husbandmen, Jesus's parabolic style of concealing the true meaning of many of His parables was thrown out of the window. The interpretation of this parable was obvious and recognized by the Jewish audience. The householder who planted the vineyard is the Father. The wicked husbandmen are the Jewish people. The servants sent to the husbandmen who beat one, and killed another, and stoned another-represented the prophets and wise men sent to the Jews. "Wherefore, behold, I send unto you prophets, and wise men, and the scribes: and some of them ye shall kill and crucify; and some of them shall ye scourge in your synagogues, and persecute them from city to city." (Matthew 23:34) When the wicked husbandmen saw the son of the householder, said among them, "This is the heir; come, let us kill him, and let us seize on his inheritance." They caught him, and cast him out of the vineyard and killed him. The son of the householder who planted the vineyard is Jesus Christ. The Jews knew immediately that the parable was directed against them. If Jesus's intention was to make the Jewish authorities angry, He succeeded. After that parable, the chief priests and the scribes sought how to lay hands on Jesus: "And the chief priests and the scribes the same hour sought to lay hands on him; and they feared the people: for they perceived that he had spoken this parable against them." (Luke 20:19)

Scene 4

Provocative Sermons in the Temple Against the Jewish Rulers

> *But woe to you, scribes, and Pharisees, hypocrites! For ye shut up the kingdom of heaven against men; for ye neither go in yourselves, neither suffer ye them that are entering to go in.*

—Matthew 23:13

The Jewish authorities were in disarray over what to do. Jesus did not make it easy for them. He kept up His public acts against the Jewish authorities to provoke them. Jesus's last speech in the Solomon's pouch recorded in chapter 23 of the Gospel of Matthew was openly directed against the Jewish authorities. It prompted the high priest to call for an emergency meeting. "Then gathered the chief priest and the Pharisees a council, and said, what do we? For this man doeth many miracles. If we let him thus alone, all men will believe on him: and the Romans shall come and take away both our place and nation And one of them, named Caiaphas, being the high priest that same year, said unto them, Ye know nothing at all Nor consider that it is expedient for us, that one man should die for the people, and that the whole nation perish not." (John 11:47–50) At that stage and time, the Jewish authorities were not thinking of crucifixion. Getting the Romans involved never crossed their minds. All they wanted was to take Jesus secretly and kill him by stoning or throw him out of the pinnacle of the temple.

Jesus staged His entry into Jerusalem, cleaned the temple, and preached in the temple to provoke the Jewish authority to act. Jesus had to be on that cross. The ubiquitous *modus operandi* of the revelation of those plans translates beyond human comprehension at that time. For generations the inability to discern the mysteries of Jesus's last visit to Jerusalem and His mutinous acts led to many misconceptions about Jesus's personality, His life, and the reason for His unique motive to return to Jerusalem to be crucified.

Believe nothing, no matter where you read it, or who said it or even if I have said it, unless it agrees with your own reason and common sense.

—Buddha

The display of multiple rebellious acts---the Mardi Gras-type parade into Jerusalem, the cleansing of the temple, the parable of the wicked husbandmen, the woes He was causing the Jewish authorities, the claim that He was Lord to King David and not his son—all those things could no longer be tolerated by the Jewish authorities. But Jesus had not yet finished provoking them. His grand master plan that would help lift Him up on the cross had not yet been revealed. He had crafted it well. The invisible Father knew about it and was watching.

Scene 5

The Authorized Mission of Judas Iscariot to the Jewish Authorities and Jesus's Arrest at Gethsemane
"What you have to do, do quickly." —Jesus said to Judas during the Last Supper. The authorized mission of Judas Iscariot, led to Jesus being lifted up on the cross. It formed an integral part of what was finished at Golgotha. Judas's authorized identification of Jesus to the mob that came to arrest Him paved the way for the completion

of Jesus's demonstration of the miracle of the earthly stages of human creation. It was not an act of treason or a betrayal of Jesus. If Jesus had failed in the demonstration of that miracle then Judas's betrayal would be considered treason. The more we dig into the sanctioned act of Judas Iscariot, the more we uncover the hidden values of that divine act. God does not assign any job to a traitor. Jesus did not select and ordain a betrayer.

Overwhelmed by our inability to gain insight into the mysteries of the planned pre-Golgotha provocative demonstrations of Jesus that led Him to the cross, the act of Judas was considered a betrayal. However, humanity must not be blamed. Who can interpret all the events that happened in Jerusalem and at Golgotha without insight into the inscrutable hidden secrets of what Jesus was doing? Without exception, all the people, including the apostles, were disappointed by the way the event ended. Today, Jesus has allowed us to look at the contents of one of the three measures of the meals, where part of the leaven was hidden. We have no reason to continue to torment the spirit of an ordained blessed apostle, Judas Iscariot.

The epically ubiquitous and extraordinary drama of the last days of Jesus was performed by people who had been assigned their roles by the Father and Jesus Christ, but they had no knowledge of what they were doing. They were not allowed to ask questions or seek explanations for many of the tasks assigned to them during the last days of Jesus in Jerusalem. The Father and His Son, Jesus Christ, had not allowed anyone to know what was going on. Jesus revealed to the apostles only what He wanted them to know.

I am certain that contacting the Jewish authorities was not Judas Iscariot's own idea. The reason is simple: Judas did not know the spiritual significance of what he was told to do quickly. "What you have to do, do quickly," Jesus said to Judas. Diligence, loyalty, humility, honesty, discipline, moral virtue, love of God and their Master, obedience to His instructions, and absolute silence to any revealed secret that they must keep to themselves, were the hall-marks of the ordained apostles. The only ones that would testify to the character of Judas Iscariot were his Master and the other apostles.

Judas knew what Jesus had instructed him to do. Whatever He told Judas to do must be kept secret. Judas obeyed and said nothing to the other apostles. It was a secret mission to be executed by the most trusted apostle. His name is Judas Iscariot, the son of Simon from the tribe of Judah! When Judas left the upper chamber to carry out the Master's command, the other apostles thought, "Because Judas had the bag that Jesus had said to him, buy those things that we have need of against the feast; or that he should give something to the poor." (John 13:29) Judas could not have gone to the Jewish authorities to reveal where Jesus was. Jesus had no reason to send Judas to reveal to the Jewish authorities where He was on the day of His arrest. The Jews knew Jesus went to the garden at the Brook of Cedron many times with His apostles. The Jewish authorities needed no one to tell them where Jesus was. Jesus was not in hiding as Jesus Himself recounted to the mob that came after Him: "Then Jesus said unto the chief priests, the captain of the temple and the elders which were come to Him, Be ye come out as against a thief with swords and staves? When I was daily with you in the temple, ye stretched forth no hands against me." (Luke 22:52–53)

Some divine appointed participants, fulfilling the most important roles in the Father's business, were incapable of discussing or explaining their actions. Therefore, it was in the case of Judas Iscariot, the son of Simon from the tribe of Judah. Judas Iscariot was an ordained apostle. He had his feet washed by Jesus and participated in the Last Supper in the upper room. He ate the bread and drank the wine that was offered to them by their Master. The gathering in the upper chamber was not to reveal to the apostles what was in God's plan that will be completed within the next two days. The Lord of secrets, Jesus Christ, disclosed nothing; such a revelation would have jeopardized the completion of the everlasting miracle

Judas had no choice. The Master commanded, and in compliance with their relationship with Him, Judas obeyed. It was Jesus, His Master, who kept everything secret. The most important question is this: what was that command that Judas must go and do quickly? If you examine the immediate reaction of the Jewish authorities when Judas delivered the message as well as the immediate reaction of the high priest Caiaphas when Jesus was tried before him, you can decipher what Judas's message was and what he was instructed to reveal to the Jewish authorities that infuriated them enough to take immediate action against Jesus.

Did Jesus reveal the same message He had instructed Judas to deliver to the Jewish authorities when He was tried before the high priest? The answer is yes. The divine command, the fifth provocative act, to reveal who His Master is and who the Father is, to the Jewish authorities, was given to the most trusted apostle. His name was Judas Iscariot, the son of Simon.

All things are delivered unto me of my Father: and no man knoweth the Son, but the Father; neither knoweth any man the Father, save the Son, and he to whomsoever the Son will reveal him.

---Matthew 11:27 Luke 10:22

It was the highest honor ever bestowed on any human being since the world began. Although Jesus's epic miracle of human creation would reveal Himself and the Father, but for what Jesus had to do to complete the demonstration of that earthly stages of human creation, He had to reveal Himself and the Father to Judas Iscariot.

However, what did Jesus reveal about Himself and His Father to Judas alone? Definitely not that He is the Christ, the Son of the living God. That was common knowledge among all the apostles.

A new revelation to Judas about Himself and His Father must have been the message conveyed to the Jewish authorities. It had nothing to do with the proof to the Jewish authorities that Jesus was the expected Jewish Messiah who would redeem Israel. The Jews did not acknowledge Jesus as the expected Jewish Messiah. Jesus never claimed to be the Jewish Messiah. I am as certain that the authorized divine command was the same thing Jesus revealed about Himself and His Father when He was tried before the high priest Caiaphas. They heard the same thing from Jesus's own mouth and call Jesus a Blasphemer who broke the first law of the Ten Commandments of Moses and had encouraged others to do so.

The message of the authorized revelation about Himself and His Father through Judas, to the Jewish authorities, touched the essence and the core of their religion. They were angered beyond control. The Jewish authorities were not able to tolerate it. What Judas revealed to the Jewish authorities evoked such indignation that they immediately sent the mob with stakes and knives to arrest Jesus. , Judas's authorized message to the Jewish authorities evoked a cascade of events that led Jesus to the cross, and to the successful completion of the miracle of the earthly phase of human creation.

CHAPTER 5

JESUS'S TRIAL AND CONDEMNATION TO DEATH BY THE JEWISH AUTHORITIES

Thou shall have no other Gods before me. —First of the Ten Commandments. Exodus 20:3 Before me no God was formed, nor there any after Me.

—Isaiah 43:10

Then cried Jesus in the temple as he taught, saying, Ye both know me, and ye know whence I am: and I am not come of myself, but he that sent me is true, whom ye know not. But I know him: for I am from him, and he hath sent me.

John 7:28-29

And the Father Himself, which hath sent me, hath borne witness of me. Ye have neither heard His voice at any time, nor seen His shape.

—Jesus. John 5:37

od, the Father, that Jesus presented, knew that the Jewish authorities–the Scribes, the members of the Sanhedrin and the Sadducees, and the Pharisees, many of them doctors of the Law-would mount an incredible antagonism to the works of Jesus and condemn Him to death, yet He sent Him to the world as a Jew. Jesus come into the world as a Jew and lived among the people that condemned Him to death? Why did Jesus choose the twelve apostles who were of Jewish origin to work with Him?

They are not of the world, just as I am not of the world.

---Jesus John 17:16

If ye were of the world, the world would love his own: but because ye are not of the world, but I have chosen you out of the world, therefore the world hateth you.

---John 15:19

If the world hates you, ye know that it hated me before it hated you.

---John 15:18

What is the reason for the hatred? The most important question is this: is Jesus Christ a Jew? It is a question that is of critical importance, not only to the Jews and the Christians, but to Muslims, Hindus, Buddhist, Confucians, Taoists, Shintoists, to all mankind whether you believe in any God or not. Why did Jesus volunteer to come down and be born as a Jew under the law that He refused to obey.

A guided insight into the mysteries of the reason why Jesus landed in Palestine as a Jew, when revealed, would end the search for any other God, but the Father of Jesus. The chief priests and the scribes and the elders also made multiple attempts to kill Jesus, but could not do so because of His popularity. (Mark 11:18, Luke19:47) After Jesus's speech on the parable of the wicked husbandman, the same group sought to seize Him. Two days before the Passover feast the chief priests and the scribes again wanted to kill him but feared the people. (Matthew 26:4, Mark 14:1, Luke 22:1) Even King Herod wanted to kill him. (Luke 13:31) If Jesus is a Jew, why were they trying to kill Him?

But now ye seek to kill me, a man that hath told you the truth.

Jesus John 8:40

The scribes and the Pharisees knew that Jesus-judging from His utterances and behavior-was not one of them. It did not take long before they knew that Jesus was not the expected Jewish Messiah or even a Prophet sent by God to fulfill His promise to Israel. The public was mesmerized by Jesus's words and power, as He performed miracles that nobody had ever performed. They wondered how a man can have such power. An excellent review on how the crowd saw Jesus is found in *The Man from Nazareth* – Harry E. Fosdick. Jesus's popularity was great that the crowd even sought to "take Him by force and make Him a king." (John 6:15) His fame had "spread everywhere throughout all the surrounding region of Galilee." (Mark 1:2)

However, the Jewish authorities were not amazed or deceived. They hated the day Jesus was born in Palestine. Today, if the reason why Jesus came to Palestine is revealed-as I have revealed in this epiphany and will continue to do so-all the Jews who believe in the God of Abraham, Isaac and Jacob, will tell all Christians who worship God, the Father of Christ to leave the land of Israel. Perhaps, the only group they may tolerate is the Jehovah witnesses who still believe in the God of Moses and Jesus but relied heavily on the Old Testament texts and on the book of Revelation for their spirituality. Simon, the just, and a devout man, saw the fate of his people when he took the infant Jesus in his arms and said;"Behold, this child is set for the fall and the rising again of many in Israel, and for a sign which shall be spoken against." (Luke 2:34)

Jesus knew why they were trying to kill Him. The Jewish authorities knew why they were trying to kill Jesus. Jesus said that he revealed the truth and for that reason, the Jews wanted to kill Him. What was that truth? What did He reveal to the Jews? Jesus was accused of many things by the Jews during His mission. Nobody would condemn a man for associating himself with sinners and the poor or for performing healing miracles on Sabbath day. Jesus's last entry into Jerusalem in a Mardi Gras parade style, His cleansing of the Temple, the parable of the two sons and the wicked husbandmen, His last speech in the Temple, (Matthew 23) were all provocative acts directed against the Jewish authorities to take immediate action against Him as to continue the works of His Father. What was that work of the Father? Jesus knew why they had planned to condemn Him to death. He knew why He was sent to the world by His Father. The Jewish authorities always had spies reporting to them all the actions and whereabouts of Jesus. Jesus did not send Judas Iscariot to reveal to the Jews where they will find Him. What did He authorize Judas to tell the Jewish authorities? They knew what Jesus was doing all the time.

Jesus was arrested after sunset at night. The mob did not try to kill Him. Before sunrise the following day, He was handed over to Pontius Pilate, to be tried in the Praetorium. There was no trial that night. The deposed High Priest Annas questioned Jesus before sending Him to the members of the Sanhedrin assembled by Caiaphas who also interrogated Him. If they sought witnesses from the mob against Jesus, what then was their reason to arrest Him?

Jesus knew about the conspiracy and the order from Pontius Pilate to arrest Him. He knew that Caiaphas would not let Him go. He had revealed to His apostles what would happen to Him in Jerusalem. During the mock trial, the High Priest Caiaphas asked Him

"Art thou the Christ? Tell us."

"If I tell you, you will not believe, nor let me go." Jesus replied

Jesus knew the Jewish authorities had no political power to arrest Him. That order to arrest Him came from the governor Pontius Pilate. There was no real trial.

The Jewish authorities did not condemn Jesus to death because He claimed to be the Son of God. That problem surfaced early during His mission and Jesus handled it well by telling them that they are also gods as was written in their Scripture.

Is it not written ye are (also) *gods?*

---Jesus

Many before Jesus and after Him called themselves the sons of God. They were not condemned to death. Under the Jewish law, it is a blasphemy to claim equality with God. That is blasphemy. Jesus was accused of blasphemy. "But for blasphemy, because you claim to be God." (John 10:33) "I and the Father are one." (John 10:31) "I am the way, and the truth and the life. No one comes to the Father except through me." (John 14:6) Was Jesus claiming to be a Mediator, bypassing Moses? Was He claiming a divine authority? Were those utterances the real reason why Jesus was condemned to death by His own people? The answer is no.

Was Jesus Christ, by proclaiming that He was sent from heaven by His Father, promoting another God, unknown to the Jews, that is not Jehovah-the God of Israel? The answer is yes. That was the truth that Jesus was revealing. Jesus refused to verbalize it bluntly, but shadowed it in many of His words on this Father, in the parables of the Kingdom of God, in His miracles and other works that He said He was able to do because of the Spirit of this Father in Him. The truth, Jesus insisted will make everyone free. (John 8:32) This is the truth as verbalized and demonstrated partially by Christ before His death, led the Jews to condemn Him to death. Jesus revealed His Father as the only true God, (John 17:3) and broke the first law of the Ten Commandments. By His miracles and words of wisdom, the people believed in Him. Jesus trained His apostles to go to all parts of the world to disseminate that information. The apostles also got involved and were considered as enemies to the Jewish religion.

Jesus, who started His work with the proclamation that the Kingdom of God was at hand, added yet another new dimension to what the Jews considered the greatest of all blasphemies. Jesus told them that they do not know anything about Him or the Father that sent Him. But that "I know Him, for I am from Him, and He hath sent me." (John 7:29) "I am one that bears witness of myself, and the Father that sent me beareth witness of me." When the Jews asked Him "Where is thy Father?" Jesus answered, "Ye neither know me, nor my Father: if ye had known me, ye should have known my Father also." (John 8:18-19) This new dimension came as a shock to members of the most resilient religion-Judaism-in the history of mankind. Jesus, for the introduction of another God that He called the Father, unknown to the Jewish nation and claiming that He had all divine authority from that new God, thereby making Himself also a God, must be put to death. To allow Jesus to continue with what He was doing would be the end of their religion and the influence of their God. Jesus, who did not, as an adult, behave like a Jew, landed in Palestine as a Jew. Did He succeed in His mission to enthrone His Father as the only true God? The answer is yes, as perceived by Jesus: "I have glorified Thee on the earth: I have finished the work which thou gave me to do." (John 17:4) This

treatise will reveal how Jesus did it. It would be no longer neces-
sary to go to Jerusalem to look for His bones or his burial clothes
as to know who Jesus is and His Father. Jesus allowed the Jews
to condemn Him to death without offering any defense and on
the cross asked His Father to forgive them because they did not
know what they were doing.

The effects of that condemnation, when revealed became the
Achilles' heel for the Jews and their God. It sets us on a platform to
have a glimpse of the spiritual world of Christ and His Father. How
many Gods are out there? Jesus said His Father is the only true
God that gives eternal life. In essence, He is the true God of creation who controls human life. "And we know that the Son of God
is come, and hath given us an understanding, that we may know
him that is true, and we are in him that is true, even in his Son
Jesus Christ. This is the true God, and eternal life." (1 John 5:20)

*But to us there is but one God, the Father, of whom are all things,
and we in him; and one Lord Jesus Christ, by whom are all things,
and we by him.*

---1 Corinthians 8:6

Marcion, a first century theologian, was the first to reveal that
Jesus introduced a new God. He called this God, the Good
God of the Father of Jesus Christ. He identified the God of Old
Testament revelations, the Jewish God, as an inferior creator
God. Marcion was labeled a heretic because the platform on
which he based his epiphany was unconvincing and his theol-
ogy of two Gods- an inferior creator God of the Old Testament
revelations and the Good God of Jesus Christ-was inconsistent
with the Jewish belief of one God and Jesus's belief of only one
true God-His Father. If the Jewish authorities believed that the
Father presented to them by Jesus Christ is the God of Israel,

they would not have mounted the mortal hostility against Jesus and His apostles. The Jews were the greatest obstacle to the growth of Christianity. The Jews were not deceived. They knew that the Father presented to them by Jesus was something new, projected in the most ubiquitous modus operandi, as to even silence the God of Israel. That would result in the loss of all the promises of –the Messiah, the Promised Land-that their God vowed to Israel and the Romans would rule them permanently. They would rather die-as they did in the past, for their God than to see Jesus destroy the Holy One of Israel. They vowed to destroy Him first. The morbid hatred was so intense that during Jesus's trial before Pontius Pilate, they accepted the consequences of their action, not only on themselves, buy also on their children.

Then answered all the people, and said, His blood be on us, and on our children.

--- Matthew 27:25

Jesus on the other hand was relentless in the proclamation of the new and only true God: His Father. He was ready to die for His Father and for His task for humanity. He must obey the will of His Father and reveal Him, not only in Palestine but in the whole world. His Father must be glorified and enthroned, not only as the only true God of the Universe who reigns and controls all things including the creation of all human beings and the world but also as the Lord of all Spirits. He had to complete the miracle of creation using Himself as example.

Jesus metaphorically called the Kingdom of God that He introduced-the new wine, and the new clothes. Jesus portrayed it in a parable; "No man putteth a piece of a new garment upon an old; if otherwise, then both the new maketh a rent, and the piece that

61

was taken out of the new agreed not with the old. And no man putteth new wine into old bottles; else the new wine will burst the bottles, and be spilled, and the bottles shall perish. But new wine must be put into new bottles; and both are preserved. No man also having drunk old wine straightway desired new: for he said, the old is better." (Luke 5:36-39) The old wine is Judaism. The trajectory of this His Kingdom of God points to His Father, to creative activities of all mankind and to His new Christianity.

What was it that Jesus said and did that alerted the Jews that the Father revealed by Jesus is not the same Jewish God that Moses revealed to the Jews? It was reported in the Old Testament literature that the God of Israel spoke to him on Mount Heron. (Exodus 3:6) Moses also received the Ten Commandments from God on Mount Sinai. The same God did not allow Moses to see His face, but allowed him to see His back. (Exodus 33:21-23) To help him liberate his people from Egypt. Moses returned to Egypt with the rod of God in his hand. (Exodus 4:20) Many prophets of Israel also said that God, the Holy One of Israel spoke to them. Then came Jesus who said, "The Father himself, which hath sent me, hath borne witness of me. Ye have neither heard his voice at any time, nor seen his shape." (John 5:37) The God that spoke to Moses and the Prophets of Israel was not the invisible Father that Jesus introduced in Palestine whose voice nobody ever heard and whose shape no one had seen. The critical question is this: whose shape did Moses see and whose voice did Moses and the Prophets hear? During his earthly life, Moses did not know of the Father that Jesus proclaimed. "All things are delivered unto me of my Father: and no man knoweth the Son, but the Father; neither knoweth any man the Father, save the Son, and *he* to whomsoever the Son will reveal *him*. (Matthew 11:27) Jesus performed miracles and did all His work with the Spirit of His Father that was in Him.

Believest thou not that I am in the Father, and the Father in me? The words that I speak unto you I speak not of myself: but the Father that dwelleth in me, he doeth the works.

---John 14:10

The Jews believed in a God you must fear—a God that protects Israel and punishes the enemies of Israel. This God makes Israel the first nation and its inhabitant's first-class citizens of this world. The God-human bondage is between this God and the Israelites. The Gentiles are excluded in that bondage, its experience, and the subsequent salvation. The Jewish people who were in the Nazarene synagogue were filled with wrath and attempted to kill Jesus when He made the revelation that salvation also belongs to the Gentiles. They were angry when Jesus reminded them that in the period of the great famine, the prophet Elias was sent to a widow who was a Gentile in Sarepta, a city of Sidon. Additionally, He told them that, in the era of the prophet Elijah, the prophet was sent to cure Naman, a Syrian, of his leprosy. The Jews were taught that salvation belongs only to the Jews and that the love of God for the Jews is the only thing that never fails. Jesus revealed a universal God, the Father that blesses and loves all people and all nations. When Jesus spoke of a God He called His Father that was quite different from the vindictive Jewish God, He sealed His fate with the Jews

What king, going to make war against another king, sitteth not down first, and consulteth whether he be able with ten thousand to meet him that cometh against him with twenty thousand?

---Luke 14:31

*How can one enter into a strong man's house, and spoil his goods,
except he first bind the strong man? And then he will spoil his house.*

---Matthew 12:29

Jesus was determined to glorify His Father and enthrone Him as
the only true God. He knew the obstacles He would face. He prepared well for His task. He knew He would win.

Jesus used the Temple (the strong man's house) as the platform to attack the Jewish religious authorities. (Matthew 23)
Jesus went to the temple and cleansed it (spoiled the goods of
the strong man), "Jesus went into the temple, began to cast out
them that sold and bought in the temple, and overthrew the
tables of the money changers and these of them that sold doves.
And would not suffer any man should carry any vessels through
the temple." (Mark 11:15–16) Probably, Jesus made attempts
to stop the animal sacrifices. Animal sacrifices for the atonement of their sins were a core element of the religion. Jesus
touched the very essence of the Jewish religious service. No Jew
would stand for it. However, by cleansing the temple, Jesus got
what He wanted. The Jewish authorities intensified their plan
to kill Jesus when they heard what He did in the temple. "And
the scribes and the chief priests heard it; they sought how they
might destroy Him." (Mark 11:18) To make the matter worse,
Jesus predicted the destruction of the Temple. But He was not
finished yet. On the moment that Jesus died on the cross, the
veil of the Temple in the Holy of the Holies of the Temple was
rent from top to bottom. The Jews have not yet rebuilt that
Temple as of today.

It was reported that Jesus said: "Think not that I am come to
destroy the law, or the prophets: I am not come to destroy, but to
fulfill." (Matthew 5:17) It depends on whose law and the prophets Jesus was referring to. Was Jesus referring to the Laws of

His Father or the Laws of the Jewish God given to the Israelites through Moses? Jesus did not come to fulfill the Laws of Moses. He came to destroy both the Ten Commandments and the Torah including the dietary laws attached to them, sparing only some of the moral and ethical laws. You cannot destroy a law by personal words. You can destroy a law by your actions that prompt others to follow. If you are looking for texts in the Gospel where Jesus said He was going to destroy the moral and ethical parts of the Ten Commandments and the Torah, you will be disappointed. Look at His words and action. Look again on His activities in the Temple at Jerusalem. You know what happened to the veil inside the Holy of the Holies the moment Jesus died. He predicted the Temple was going to be destroyed and did nothing to save it. The Sabbath is the Jewish day of rest, the seventh day of the Hebrew week. It is commanded by their God to be kept holy as the day He rested from His creation. (Exodus 20:8) Jesus broke that law by healing the sick and allowing His apostles to pluck corns on a Sabbath day. (Luke 6:1-10) When challenged, Jesus insisted that His Father that sent Him works every day; therefore He too, works every day. Jesus's Father Works on Sabbath days, but the Jewish God does not work on Sabbath days. There was not a single Jewish Law that Jesus obeyed and warned His apostles to beware of leavens (the doctrines) of the Pharisees and the Sadducees. (Matthew 16:6-12) The law that Jesus came to fulfill was the Laws and Commandments of His Father. "For verily I say unto you, till heaven and earth pass, one jot or one tittle shall in no wise pass from the law, till all be fulfilled. Whosoever therefore shall break one of these least commandments, and shall teach men so, he shall be called the least in the kingdom of heaven: but whosoever shall do and teach them, the same shall be called great in the kingdom of heaven. For I say unto you, that except your righteousness shall exceed the righteousness of the scribes and Pharisees, ye shall in no case enter into the kingdom of heaven." (Matthew 5:18-20) The laws of His

Father and Jesus's commandments exceed what was prescribed by the God of Israel through Moses for the people of Israel.

As an adult, Jesus refused to offer any sacrifice in the Temple and was constantly challenging the High Priest and members of the Sanhedrin. He knew the strength of the Jewish authorities and the core foundation of the Jewish faith-the Ten Commandments and the Law and destroyed them, sparing only the moral and the ethical segments. Jesus would say to His audience: "You have heard that it was said by them of old time…... But I say unto you…" Jesus was not referring to the Jewish Prophets of old time when He said "Think not that I am come to destroy the law, or the prophets: I am not come to destroy, but to fulfill." He had already destroyed them when He announced publically that no one ever heard the voice of His Father. You begin to wonder whose voice the Prophets of Israel heard. Jesus and His Father have their own Laws and Prophets. "Wherefore, behold, I send unto you prophets, and wise men, and scribes: and some of them ye shall kill and crucify; and some of them shall ye scourge in your synagogues, and persecute them from city to city." (Matthew 23:34) The twelve apostles were treated in a similar fashion. Eleven of them were murdered.

Jesus had the courage to tell Judaism not to evaporate or to step aside, but to come inside the capsule of what He brought down from His Father: His Kingdom of God. That was impossible for the Jews. To do so would mean to abandon the God that Moses revealed to them, and the Torah and the hope for the Messiah. Today Jesus is still calling on them and all current forms of Christianity as is pre-scribed, proclaimed and practiced today to stop all activities that leave Christians wondering like sheep without shepherd, to come inside the capsule of His kingdom of God. When both are inside, the whole world would be attracted and they too would come in-side. This is the main objective of the Christianity of Christ: to bring all the people of the world, under one fold. This is in es-sence, the goal of Jesus's Kingdom of God. A house divided cannot stand. Such division brings nothing but indifference to evil and the sufferings of mankind, injustice, uncontrolled hatred, monstrous wars, more refugees, and ignorance of who we are.

Some of the Jewish people liked what Jesus proclaimed and followed Him everywhere. The Jewish authorities were not deceived. Even King Herod joined in mounting the mortal opposition to Jesus. Jesus was warned "to get out, and depart for Herod will kill thee." (Luke 13:31) Do you not want to know why Paul, before his conversion, said as he defended himself against the Jews said: "And I persecuted this way unto the death, binding and delivering into prisons both men and women. As also the high priest doth bear me witness, and all the estate of the elders: from whom also I received letters unto the brethren, and went to Damascus, to bring them which were there bound unto Jerusalem, for to be punished." (Acts 22:4-5) The reason why the Jewish authorities and Paul were persecuting those people is this: Jesus introduced a new God that He called His Father and many people believed in Him and His message.

The *mysterium tremendum et fascinans* (mystery that is fearful and fascinates) to me is that perhaps the popularity of the Jewish God and the God that controls the Roman people attracted Jesus to come down to Palestine and reveal His Father-the only true God-who reigns and controls all things. That all along from the beginning, the Father and Himself, have been creating human beings and control all their activities. That Jesus's timeless demonstration of the miracle of the earthly stages of human creation was the platform the Father and Jesus Christ used to reveal the human creative trajectory of all mankind-including the Jews, that we may believe in them. Jesus stressed this belief in His Father and in Him as the core element in all His words and works. To continue this display of proof, to save and control what the Father and Himself are creating from other Spirits, Jesus must be condemned to death by the Jews and crucified by the Romans. The façade of the events of this human creative trajectory is breath-taking. Jesus was excited about it.

> *Then cried Jesus in the temple as he taught, saying, Ye both know me, and ye know whence I am: and I am not come of myself, but he that sent me is true, whom ye know not. But I know him: for I am from him, and he hath sent me.*

---John 7:28-29

We must give credit to the Egyptian Pharaoh Akhenaten, who ruled Egypt for seventeen years and died in BC 1336. He was the first to introduce the concept of one God who controls all things. He was sure that one day that God would manifest Himself to the world. That prophesy was fulfilled through Jesus Christ.

The divine authority Jesus claimed and publicized to the people about His Father and Himself, was a challenge to the Jewish religion and their God. It evoked a lethal weapon that was used to send Jesus to the cross. Jesus's love for the Jewish people that He encountered remained pure and holy, even His opponents said so, however, for introducing a new God that He called His Father and for claiming to be a God, He was condemned to death. The Father who sent Jesus to Palestine allowed it to happen.

CHAPTER 6

JESUS ALLOWED THE ROMANS TO CRUCIFY HIM

The trial of Jesus before the Roman-appointed procurator Pontius Pilate was the last planned provocative act of Jesus. It was critical event in Jesus's miracle of the earthly stages of human creation. It enabled Jesus to be "lifted up" on the cross. Jesus used silence, arrogance, and stubbornness—the antithesis of His teachings with metaphoric expression on the truth-as tools which confused the governor. It was done under the influence and power of the invisible God as was reported in the Gospel. Pilate had said to Jesus. "Speaketh thou not unto me? Knowest thou not that I have the power to crucify thee, and have the power to release thee," Jesus replied. "Thou couldest have no power at all against me, except it were given unto thee from above." (John 19:10–11) What happened during the trial had been predetermined by His Father. Jesus must be "lifted up" on the cross and be crucified for the execution of the everlasting miracle of the earthly stages of human creation.

During the trial, Pontius Pilate categorically stated, "I find no fault in Him," yet he delivered Jesus to be crucified with the help of the Roman soldiers. Pontius Pilate had no power

69

at all over Jesus. The power of the almighty God controlled all things. Although Pilate found no fault in Jesus, it was Caesar's appointee's fate to condemn Him to be crucified. The reported trial of Jesus by Pontius Pilate was a sham. First, Jesus was taken to the Praetorium, the official residence of Pontius Pilate and the administrative headquarter of the Roman garrison. The comparison of it today is the Pentagon. How many Jews do you think that the Roman soldiers allowed into that compound on that day? Probably only the band and the officers and the captains that arrested Him were allowed to enter the Praetorium. Second, the most important question is this: why did Pontius Pilate order the crucifixion when he found no fault in Jesus? All the attorneys and all who are spiritually awake want to know the answer. He did question Jesus and wanted to know if He is the King of the Jews. But that would not constitute a trial. There was no trial. The heartless, corrupt Roman appointed governor had ordered the execution of Jesus by crucifixion before Jesus was arrested and handed over to him in the Praetorium. Caiaphas, Annas and some members of the Sanhedrin that knew of the plan could not refuse. If they refuse to arrest Jesus, then, "the Romans will come and take away our place and nation." One man had to die that the whole nation of Israel should not perish. That man was Jesus Christ.

I have always wondered why Jesus came into the world when the Romans ruled the world and had enthroned their Gods and Goddesses as divine to be worshipped in their Empire. Never before, in the history of humankind has any one group, as the Romans, collected so many idols that people worship with passion and deep devotion. Those gods and goddesses had entrenched themselves and had an influence on the minds of the people of Rome and those that Rome governed. With all His powers and authority, Jesus allowed them to crucify Him. What is the reason behind this? At first glance, we may think that Pontius Pilate was in charge. Jesus and His Father completely directed that scene in this second Act of the epic miracle. They simply allowed it to happen.

Jesus did not come to the world to be crucified by the Romans to wipe away the sins of the world or quell the wrath of God for the sins we committed against Him, including the original sin of Adam and Eve. The crucifixion and the death of Jesus was a stage in the miracle of the earthly phase of human creation. Jesus used Himself as a model. It was also a platform-as I revealed in my book *the Father's Business and the Spiritual cross*- that Jesus used to silence the Gods and Goddesses of the Greco Roman Empire and other Gods. The cross became the Achilles' heel for Rome and the people of the Empire. Subsequently, the glorified Spirit of risen Christ illuminated many hearts and awakened the divine potency of human souls, including the souls of the Emperors and Roman people who sentenced and crucified Him. Emperor Constantine became a Christian in 312 AD. Their Gods and Goddesses were silenced and their temples destroyed. Today Rome has become a holy city of God with the enclosed Vatican City as the capital of the largest Christian community. This is one of the mysteries of Golgotha. This is a mystery that was hidden in Jesus's performance of the everlasting miracle of the earthly stages of human creation. Today, Jesus's Kingdom of God continues to power this miracle in human souls and the spiritualization of human souls continued without the colossal obstacles mounted by the spirits that influenced the Romans to build temples and worship them as gods and goddesses. Jesus marched on to Golgotha, and was determined that He must not fail, as everything depended on Him.

I have a baptism to be baptized with; and how am I straitened till it be accomplished.

—Luke 12:50

CHAPTER 7

JESUS DIED AS A HUMAN BEING AT GOLGOTHA

For many deceivers are entered into the world, who confess
not that Jesus Christ is come in the flesh. This is a deceiver
and an antichrist.

2 John 1:7

What was Jesus Christ doing on this planet as a human being? First ask yourself: what are you doing on this planet as a human being? If we really want to know why Jesus died as one of us, we must also ask: why do we all have to die as humans? If you ask Joseph and Mary, who Jesus is, they will tell you that He is our son. Jesus on many occasions called Himself the Son of man-the Son of a man. This title must not be confused with the apocalyptic 'Son of Man' expressions in the books of Daniel 8:17, Ezekiel 2:1 and other Jewish literatures. The comprehension why Jesus was born like us and the usefulness of that information in moving forward must be dissociated from all the concepts of the Son of Man in the Jewish literature. The knowledge of Jesus as a human being, gives us insight to know what the Father and Jesus Christ are doing for the people of the world. When projected against the background of

Jesus's Kingdom of God that came, the spiritual events at Golgotha, and His resurrection, the façade of the human creative trajectory is revealed. That revelation carries with it the enthronement of His Father as the only true Creator God and Himself also as a Creator and a God.

Jesus's willingness to obey the will of His Father was impeccable and beyond reproach. Humiliated, spat upon, scorned, scourged, stripped almost naked, and mocked, yet He was determined to drink from the cup the Father had given Him. Jesus, without offering any resistance, allowed the Jewish authorities to condemn Him to death and the Romans to nail Him on the cross. The Gospel of John reported that when Jesus had received the vinegar that was offered to Him, said, "It is finished:" and died. The Gospel records of Matthew and Mark reported that at the ninth hour, Jesus cried out with a loud voice and died. The Gospel of Like reported that when Jesus had cried out with a loud voice, He said, "Father, into Thy hands I commend my spirit." Jesus then bowed His head and died.

The Father had prevailed in what He had planned and was pleased in what Jesus finished at Golgotha. His supreme authority was revealed because He had controlled all the actions of all the earthly inhabitants who participated: the authorized divine initiative of the blessed ordained apostle Judas Iscariot, the injustice of the Roman governor, the deep hatred of the Jewish authorities, the ignorance of the Jewish mob, and the unquestioned, wicked obedience of the Roman soldiers who obeyed orders and crucified Jesus.

The mystery of Golgotha is mind boggling. However, to understand it, one has to have been following Jesus from the very beginning of His mission. It is rooted in the Kingdom of God that came, the humanity of Jesus and the work Jesus came to do for His Father and for mankind. The humanity of Jesus pierce though that inscrutable mystery of the everlasting miracle of the earthly stages of human creation and opens the portal of knowledge of the mysteries of His kingdom of God, why Jesus died, what human life is all about and the destiny of human souls. It points itself to His Father, to that one promise of the Father for mankind, to the promise of Jesus Christ to His Father and to the showcase display of what the Father and Jesus Christ are creating. It bypassed all the prophetic visions and the supposed nature of Jesus in the Old Testaments texts. It revealed a story that is our story and a future that is our future. It points to death, not as an evil event, but as a grand station on the trajectory of human creation. We too, must prepare to die as to be participants in the promised glory. The story of the humanity of Jesus, who with outstretched hands pointed to his audience as His sisters, brothers and mothers, became our story of Jesus as our brother.

The humanity of Jesus is the lens through which we see ourselves in His miracle of the earthly stages of human creation. Jesus's Kingdom of God was launched in His human soul with the Spirit of God, His Father. Jesus's Kingdom of God within us also launched with the Spirit of the Father in Christ. For the demonstration of that creative process as demonstrated in the everlasting miracle, Jesus had to be born as one of us and die as one of us that we may believe in Him and in the Father as the Lords of creation and have a guided insight into the mystery of human life. If Jesus was not born and did not die as a human being, then what He demonstrated for us would be of no value on the ground that only divine beings can accomplish such transcendental transformation. The stage everlasting miracle of human creation as orchestrated by Christ is rooted in human souls. It is also our miracle of life. If Jesus demonstrated it using Himself as an example, He had to use His human nature in the miracle. It gives mankind the assurance that we too can be participants in such miracles, not of creating others but as participants in our own creation.

Jesus was condemned to death by the Jewish authorities and crucified on the cross by the Romans. The death of Jesus represents the spiritual human creative grand station mankind must pass through to advance to its fuller destiny. Jesus was sent down to demonstrate this process to all. The cross is still holding a deep mystery of the Father-Jesus Christ human creation. If we are to penetrate into what the cross had held back for centuries and refused to let go, we must look again at that one promise of the Father to mankind-Jesus's Kingdom of God- and what Jesus continued to do with the Spirit that He got from the Father. As we move forwards, this inscrutable mystery will cease to be so if you still remember that Jesus went to Golgotha as a human being, with the Spirit of the Father in Him and has been giving this Spirit of the Father in Him-the Christ Spirit-to as many as believe in the Father and in Him. To drink the water of everlasting life, you must prepare to die with the Jesus's kingdom of God within you. That preparation is only the beginning of the long journey to eternal life.

All along the way, we have looked at the cross and found the solution to our sins and to the evil of the world instead of looking at it as a platform in our own creative trajectory to spiritual life. We look at it and found Jesus who took the punishment for us by dying on the cross to please an angry God who would have nothing to do with us until we are redeemed by the death of Christ. The wages of sin is not physical or spiritual death. We must accept that we do not know how the Father and Jesus Christ judge. Mankind fears death and considers it to be evil. The gross misunderstanding of death as "the sting of death" as punishment for our sins is an obstacle to the comprehension of the will of the Father to Jesus. We must we not be afraid to participate in this creative process that is still going on. We must not be afraid to die with Jesus's Kingdom of God within us. This creative process is irrepressible and mankind has no control of it.

CHAPTER 8

THE MYSTERIES OF JESUS'S RESURRECTION REVEALED

*Therefore doth my Father love me, because I lay down
my life, that I might take it again. No man taketh it (my
life) from me. However, I lay it down of myself. I have
the power to lay it down and I have the power to take it
again. This commandment have I received of my Father.*

John 10:17–18

I t is reasonable to assume that the above commandment from
His Father was given to Jesus before He came to the world. What
the eyewitnesses saw on the day Jesus rose from the dead was that
amazing, marvelous great work the Father had shown Jesus how
to do. That extraordinary miraculous work was His resurrection.
Jesus gave a public demonstration of it in executing the earthly
phase of human creation by resurrecting Himself. "Verily, verily,
I say unto you, the Son can do nothing of Himself, but what He
seeth the Father do: for what things soever He doeth, these also
doeth the Son likewise. The Father loved the Son and showed Him
all things that Himself doeth: and He will show Him greater works

than these that ye may marvel. For as the Father raiseth up the dead, and quickeneth them; even so the Son quickeneth whom He will." (John 5: 19-21) The Father resurrects. Jesus likewise resurrects. The amazing work in that grand demonstration is this: Jesus used Himself as a model in that miracle and in doing so, revealed the infinite power of His Kingdom of God. Jesus said: "I have the power to lay it down (*His life*) and I have the power to take it again."

Jesus, who called Himself the Lord of Resurrection, resurrected Himself in that tomb. He first had to report to His Father. It was not the Father who resurrected Jesus. If that were the case, Jesus would not have told Mary Magdalene that He had first to present Himself to the Father before she could touch Him. When Jesus perceived that Mary was about to touch Him, said, "Touch Me not, for I am not yet ascended to my Father; and to my God, and your God."

The resurrection of Jesus was a grandstand epic display of Act 3 of the greatest of all His miracles. All along, since His proclamation of the Kingdom of God that came, Jesus was executing a public exhibition of that miracle and revealing the mysteries of His Kingdom of God and no one took notice of what was going on. It was a miracle no one had attempted before, not in heaven or on earth. It is true that what was revealed on Easter was indeed the image of the risen Christ. The big question is this: did Jesus come to the world to show us that He had the power to resurrect Himself and did the cross finally on the third day after the death of Christ give up all its mysteries? The resurrection of Christ is more than the appearance of the risen glorified image of Jesus. Behind that image are more hidden treasures of the cross. Hidden behind that image are all the mysteries of Jesus's Kingdom of God, its ultimate power and why His Father sent Him to this world. Behind that image are the mysteries of human creation and the prototype of the fully spiritual human beings. Behind that image, the invisible Father became visible. Behind that image, who Jesus is, started to unfold. Behind that image, the invisible spiritual world of Jesus Christ and His Father became visible to all who have the experience of His Kingdom of God. A significant scene in the final Act of the three-staged everlasting miracle of human creation was exhibited on that day. Although the resurrection of Jesus was the strongest public display of the proof of His works and words, the most important practical exhibition of the evidence that revealed Jesus Christ and where He came from, His Father, Jesus's Kingdom of God within us, who we are and why we are here are hidden behind the image of the risen Christ. These are the fascinating mysteries of Jesus's miracle of human creation that manifested by His resurrection. However, the best scene of that miracle is yet to come.

The apostle Peter looked at the resurrection of Christ as a lively hope for mankind. "Blessed be the God and Father of our Lord Jesus Christ, which according to His abundant mercy hath begotten us again unto a lively hope by the resurrection of Jesus Christ from the dead." (1 Peter 1:3) Paul saw it as "God was in Christ reconciling the world to Himself." (2 Corinthians 5:19) The apostle John, who witnessed the whole miracle from the beginning, was sure that when Christ shall appear again, we shall be like Him. "Behold, what manner of love the Father had bestowed on us, that we be called the sons of God, therefore the world knows us not, because it knew Him not. Behold, now that we are the sons of God and it does not yet appear what we shall be, but we know that when He shall appear, we shall be like Him." (1 John 3:1-2) What Jesus did in the execution of the miracle of human creation was to use Himself as a model demonstration that gave a proof, beyond scientific methods, not of "the lively hope" or "what we shall be when He shall appear" but of the transcendental transformation of human creation with the revelation of the prototype of the spiritual image of the created human spirit. The truth is that the prototype of that image was exhibited by the showcased image of the risen

Christ. People are being resurrected every moment in His image. He came back on the fiftieth day after His ascension on the day of the Pentecost and provided imprints to human souls for the perpetual continuation of human creation to its glorious end as planned by His Father. The creation of mankind in His image is happening now. It is not an event that will occur as Paul suggested, with apocalyptic view: "when the Lord himself shall descend from heaven with a shout, with the voice of the archangel, and with the trump of God: and the dead in Christ shall rise first: then we which are alive and remain shall be caught up together with them in the clouds, to meet the Lord in the air: and so shall we ever be with the Lord." (1 Thessalonians 4:16-17) Christ is here. The Lord is not going to descend "from heaven with a shout." It is happening now. As Paul advanced in his knowledge of Christ and his experience of the 'Christ in him', he found himself in the Jesus's epic miracle of human creation, not as a future event but as an event that already occurred:

> *I am crucified with Christ: nevertheless I live; yet not I, but Christ lives in me: and the life which I now live in the flesh I live by the faith of the Son of God, who loved me, and gave himself for me.*

> ---Galatians 2:20

Paul, in his post-Damascus experience manifested the life of Christ. This is the mystery behind Paul's 'Christ in me and 'I in Christ.' In essence, Paul bore the trade mark of Jesus's kingdom of God that empowered his miracles, his knowledge of Christ, and his assurance that he participated in Jesus's miracle of human creation that made him a new creature.

How can it be that the entire mankind will be in the image of the risen Christ after resurrection? This revealed mystery of the resurrection is in conformity with what the apostle John said that 'we shall be like Him. 'The only difference is that the apostle John twittered it with apocalyptic flavor-when He (the Christ) shall appear. The Father sent Jesus as a human being to demonstrate what they have been doing all along-spiritualization of the souls of human species-created from water as males and females-with the Spirit of the Father through Christ. Jesus had said that we are born of water and of Spirit. The resurrection of the spiritualized souls after death is still going on now. "For as the Father raised up the dead, and quickened them; even so the Son quickened whom He will." (John 5: 21)

The answer to the monumental interpretation of the concept of human creation lies in the understanding of Jesus's great everlasting miracle of human creation that connected with His resurrection. Jesus's Kingdom of God powered all His miracles. The earthly phase of human creation demonstrated by Jesus has been going on before He was sent down. What was showcased at His resurrection that Mary was not allowed to touch is the prototype of the future new spiritual mankind that will end up with the godlike nature of the risen Christ. The intrinsic power of the new creature is already within you. The resurrection of Christ is the public exhibition of the miracle of human creation: the story of your journey to eternal life. It is a façade that reveals that morality, good ethics of all religions as only outward coatings of what is needed to take a quantum leap into that life. The core element of what is needed to take that transcendental quantum jump through resurrection is to drink the water of everlasting life: to enter into Jesus's Kingdom of God. This is the will of His Father.

Behold, now that we are the sons of God and it does not yet appear what we shall be, but we know that when He shall appear, we shall be like Him.

---1 John 3: 2

Jesus Christ was sent down to this world as a human being, He died as a human being. He resurrected Himself to the image of a spiritual human being. We have always assumed that as revealed by John that "when He shall appear, we shall be like Him." Do not bet on that. We do not know what Jesus and His Father look like before Jesus came. No one had seen their shape or even heard their voice before Jesus came. That Jesus came as a human being does not mean that He looks like a human being in His place of origin. The twelve apostles who "are not of this world" never saw their Master in the place from where He came. It is for this reason that Jesus prayed and petitioned to His Father: "I will that they also, whom thou hast given me, be with me where I am; that they may behold my glory, which thou has given me; for thou loves me before the foundation of the world." (John 17:24) Jesus predicted that He will be crucified and be resurrected on the third day. My dear reader, the resurrection of Jesus allowed you to have a glimpse of the creative ability of Christ and His Father and to see the prototype of your spiritual image in the creative trajectory after resurrection. It did not provide a venue for us to have a glimpse of the shape or image of Christ where He is now with His Father. That image of Jesus Christ or the Father has never been revealed to any earthly human being. Jesus did not ask Mary Magdalene not to touch Him as to show the Father His original image. His Father was accustomed to that image before the foundation of the world. Jesus was proud of the image of the prototype of the new spiritual human creature that He created using Himself as a model and wanted to show that to His Father. The Father and Jesus Christ have been creating human beings. However, *this modus operandi* used by Christ was new on the ground that Jesus stepped out of His place of origin to demonstrate the earthly stages of human creation. Jesus came down as a human being, probably not in His original shape, died and recreated Himself as a spiritual human being and was proud to present to the Father what He did. The resurrection scene in Jesus's exhibition of the final act in His miracle of the earthly of human creation educed an effect that never happened in the creative history of mankind. This is one of the deep mysteries of Jesus's epic miracle of human creation.

Jesus's resurrection was the platform that He used to demonstrate God's plan enacted with that one gift His Father gave to mankind: the gift of His Spirit. Seeing is better than imagination. The visual imagery of the risen Christ must be rooted on what God had planned all along for mankind: eternal life by His creative power of Jesus Kingdom of God The epistemology of Jesus's resurrection, gave us a glimpse into the mysteries of the Kingdom of God that came, His death and His creative power with the Spirit of God in Him. If you know that this is the truth that will set you free, will you kill what the Father is creating? Will you hate people and be jealous of them? Will you help produce weapons of mass destruction? What would you do for humanity? We must treat each other as members of the human race that the Father and Jesus Christ are creating. By His resurrection, Jesus was not only able to imprint His name in the hearts of humans forever, but He also has profound influence on human activities so that we may continue to be active participants in the Father's business. Paul's justification by faith in the risen Jesus modeled all his activities. It became the trademark of his work, the hallmark of his religion, and the culture of his deep spiritualism.

> *And this is the Father's will which hath sent me, that of all which he hath given me I should lose nothing, but should raise it up again at the last day.*

> ---John 6:39

The Father gave Jesus all of us, not just the apostles or people who call themselves Christians. Jesus's grand ambition is to kindle all hearts with the fire of His Kingdom and resurrect everyone if we are willing. His resurrection was connected and is connected to many resurrections in the past, today and will be in future. Jesus is being resurrected every day in human hearts. His Kingdom of God is growing despite all the human obstacles. The resurrection of Christ was a display of the prototype of God's new creature. I call it new because we have never seen such before. To use Himself as a model in the epic miracle was also new to the Father and Jesus Christ. Although they were creating spiritual beings before Jesus was sent down what Jesus did was a new type of miracle for this simple reason: in this once upon a time public exhibition of miracle of human creation. Jesus used Himself as the model. This is the mystery of the miracle of Jesus's resurrection, enacted with the power His Kingdom of God.

Father, I have glorified Thee on the earth: I have finished the work which you gave me to do.

---Jesus. John 17:4

My Father loves me, because I lay down my life, that I might take it again.

---Jesus. John 10:19

We look forward to our moment so that when we are resurrected; our glorified spirits will come forth with power and all the blessings of God for our manifestation in His glorified image and likeness. This is our guaranteed glory. This is the will of God for all mankind as was demonstrated in the everlasting miracle of the earthly phase of human creation that Jesus executed. The exploration of Jesus's resurrection will continue in the chapter on Easter. When I was in high school, I was mesmerized in mathematics, on how to calculate the stopping distance of a speeding vehicle when the break is applied. Jesus's epic miracle of human creation represented that speeding vehicle. Resurrection represented the time when the brake was applied. But the vehicle is still moving. The resurrection of Christ was not the end of the exhibition of the everlasting miracle. It continued to evolve at the pace determined by the Father of Christ. What subsequently happened on the day of Pentecost, provide more proof of the control of that Miracle by His Father; the evidence of the existence of that Father; validation of the divine authenticity of Jesus's words and works and Jesus divine origin. It provided the map to the final destiny of all the new created spiritual creatures and gave mankind an insight into the spiritual worlds of Christ and His Father, our God.

CHAPTER 9

THE NEW EASTER EXPERIENCE AND THE TRIUMPHANT GLORY OF JESUS'S KINGDOM

"To this end was I born, And for this cause came I unto the world."

The year was in 2002. The local newspaper in the city of Columbus Georgia, *Ledger Enquirer*, put up the ad for essay competition on 'What Easter means to me' Competitors were limited to three hundred words. Easter celebration is the most important event for Christianity. I had just published my book on *the Innocent Blood and Judas Iscariot*. I was of the impression that I know all about the resurrection of Jesus Christ and what Easter means to me and others. My essay made it to the top of those that were published. Below is a summary of what I submitted that was published:

"The real Spirit of Easter is faith in the risen Christ, in His Gospel of Redemption, in His New Covenant, and with it hopes for salvation. By His resurrection, Jesus was glorified and His divine nature revealed. That heavenly everlasting sign, Jesus's death and rebirth, also revealed the nature and supreme power of His Father. The promised gift of the Holy Ghost was made possible by His resurrection. It gives believers hope in Christ and with it access to God. It was a fulfillment of Christ's promise of the authentic life after death."

Today, I have advanced my knowledge on eternal life and on what Easter means to us in today's world. I was not satisfied with Easter faith as I believed at that time and still proclaimed by many Christians today. For many years my attempts to discover what Easter means to us seemed hopeless. It is a topic that I explored in my last two published books. As I listened to many sermons on Easter Sundays and watch human activities on that day, I was more convinced we are missing something vital. Every year, the Christians celebrate the Easter with the same message that:

Christ rose from the dead

We will be resurrected after death to inherit eternal life

He will come again to establish His kingdom on this earth.

Thereafter is the usual Easter egg hunt for the children and Easter brunch for the families. Then it is all over and we look forward to the next Easter. We go back doing what we do best: work to put food on the table; pay mortgage, educate the children, take a vacation, plan for retirement; wait for Jesus, the Messiah, to come and establish His Kingdom here or take us to Heaven. Meanwhile why we wait for Christ to come back, we manifest what He did for us with hatred, extreme greed, hypocrisy, racism, injustice, selling holy waters and abusing poor people. Then the inevitable happens-we die and hope to be resurrected by the risen Christ to a better life in heaven to live with Him forever. The foundation of that belief and proclamation came from Paul and early Christians.

For if we have been planted together in the likeness of his death, we shall be also in the likeness of His resurrection.

---Paul. Romans 6:5

It has been acclaimed that the resurrection of Jesus, celebrated as Easter was a great miracle. Indeed, it was a great miracle. Jesus's Kingdom of God featured prominently in all His miracles. Without its power, Jesus could not have performed any miracle. The problem of the interpretation of that miracle of human creation, using the resurrection as the only platform, isolated mankind to a distant future after death and removed human souls and Jesus's Kingdom of God from that great miracle. Jesus's three staged everlasting miracle of human creation was simply called the great miracle of resurrection, celebrated as Easter. The Easter Faith was transplanted to Easter Hope that all who were dead in sin, and believe in Christ would be redeemed and be resurrected by Him after the final judgment. The gross misinterpretation of death as consequences of sin and the gross misinformation on the death of Jesus as atonement and an act of redemption, served as an impenetrable smoke screen that blurred the correct interpretation of Jesus's miracle of human creation. If the Christians cannot find themselves in the everlasting miracle and in Jesus's Kingdom of God, till after we have all died, we cannot expect those who are not Christians to believe in the resurrection of Jesus.

However, to limit your experience of the miracle of Easter as is currently proclaimed with the hope that when we die, we shall be resurrected to be with the risen Christ, is not the whole truth. Resurrection of Jesus was not just an illustration of human survival after death. Jesus's everlasting miracle of the earthly stages of human creation revealed something very spectacular about Easter. The resurrection of Jesus was the most significant scene in that miracle that started with His proclamation of the Kingdom of God that came.

In order to grasp fully the meaning of Easter, we need to look at the power of Jesus's Kingdom of God. We need to remember the objectives and goals of that Kingdom. We have always to remember that the same Kingdom of God, proclaimed two thousand years ago, is still within us. (Luke 17:21) We need to explore the whole spectrum of His miracle of the earthly stages of human creation from the first to the last act and examine the proof of human creation demonstrated by Christ in that miracle. The miracle did not start or end with the resurrection of Jesus. The final scene of that miracle was showcased on the day of Pentecost. Jesus was sent by His Father to reveal to the world, through that epic miracle of human creation, the authentic proof of His creative ability with the power of the Spirit of the Father in Him (Jesus's Kingdom of God). This is the same Kingdom of God that is within us. However, we are not aware of the power of that kingdom within us. We all have the same thing that Christ gave to the apostles and Paul. It was for that reason that the Father sent Jesus as a human being to reveal to us power of His creative Spirit within us; how to use it and participate in the earthly stages of our own creation. With the Kingdom of God within us, we are portrayed in that miracle. What we celebrate as Easter was a significant scene in that miracle. We can confidently develop our own glorified Easter experience and not relegate it only to the apostles who instantaneously restored the fellowship with their risen Master when Jesus, on the day of His resurrection revealed Himself to them. Jesus, by His epic miracle of human creation, demonstrated the strongest evidence of that creative power that is inherent in all human souls and the divine origin of all His words and works.

The veil that hid the true meaning of Easter was lifted, when I recovered from the Gospel, the true meaning of Jesus's Kingdom of God within us and the power it carries along with it was revealed. It was the secret key that unlocked the deeper mysteries of that Kingdom when projected on both the Easter Faith and our Easter Experience with the risen Christ. The encrypted mysteries of Jesus's Kingdom of God allowed us to understand the full spectrum of all the three stages of Jesus's everlasting miracle of human creation. The resurrection of Jesus was the most dynamic important scene of that miracle that revealed the glorious earthly phase of Jesus's everlasting miracle of human creation. This is the glory of Easter. It was an event that revealed the ultimate power of the kingdom of God that came. It manifested the infinite glory of that Kingdom that came and is within us. It was an event that made possible the grandiose display of the final scene of Jesus's epic miracle of human creation on the day of Pentecost that was witnessed by the Jews and many people from the Roman Empire.

And he said unto them, Verily I say unto you, That there be some of them that stand here, which shall not taste of death, till they have seen the kingdom of God come with power.

---Jesus. Mark 9:1

Resurrection of Jesus revealed the best kept secret of the cross. The victory of what was finished at Golgotha is celebrated as Easter today. But what is that victory? If all you can get from the history of the death and resurrection of Jesus is that He rose from the dead on the third day after His death on the cross, then you were outside the theater where the greatest miracle ever staged on this planet was performed by Jesus Christ, the Master of miracles. Behind the cross are Paul's "unsearchable riches of Christ and the love of God that passes all understanding." Resurrection of Jesus without our finding ourselves in it is of no value to us. Human souls are involved in it and are full participants in all the stages of the epic miracle. It was for this that Jesus came as a human being. In essence, what Jesus demonstrated, by using Himself as a human being, provided mankind the evidence that we can be involved the same way in the miracle of human creation with Jesus's Kingdom of God within us if we are willing. That would constitute our Easter experience with the risen Christ. That is the victory of what was finished at Golgotha. Celebrate that victory with everyone. The Spirit of the Father is involved and is permanently in it. The Spirit of Christ is involved in it. It directed and would continue to direct all the activities of that staged miracle of human life. This information is vital because what are involved in that miracle are the spiritual components of Jesus's Kingdom of God that carries with it the coded information on who is Jesus, the nature of the Father, the nature of God's Spirit in our souls and the divine elements of eternal life. The miracle not only revealed the infinite power of Jesus's Kingdom of God, but also opened the door of that Kingdom to reveal the Paradise of true human consciousness, forgiveness, love that extends to the enemy, compassion and mercy. It provided the protean passwords to the mysteries of what was finished at Golgotha that was showcased on Easter as a very significant event in the final act in the epic exhibition of human creation. Jesus allowed Himself to be condemned by the Jewish authorities and crucified by the Romans as to achieve His goals. It was a mission bound for glory that translated into the Paradise of the human souls and glory for His Father.

Easter should be the triumphant celebration, commemorating the glorification of the risen Christ and the human experience of the glorified Spirit within us that transcended into full expression of new spiritual status as new creatures. If we are not right now involved in our earthly segment of eternal life in that experience with Jesus's Kingdom of God within us, the proclaimed Easter faith by the Christians and their leaders that that are rooted in recounting the Passion of Christ, observation of Lent with its daily Lenten devotional would be of no value to us. The merchants used the lack of knowledge of that experience to enrich themselves. The Christians in China are only a minority. However, the Chinese capitalize on our ignorance of the real Easter experience to make billions of dollars every year exporting Easter merchandise to all parts of the world. Easter experience should simply be the experience of Jesus Kingdom of God within us, connecting it with His resurrection and human creative activities as was demonstrated in His miracle of human creation. You have to have experience of that Kingdom as to have Easter experience. That experience was what was precisely exemplified by the epitome of Jesus's earthly life, the life examples of the apostles, Paul, early Christians, the late Martin Luther King and the late President Nelson Mandela. Additionally, all who did everything in their power to stop slavery-both whites and Afro-Americans-who did everything without violence to stem racism in America; and all who finally turned around and saw the evils of colonizing other nations and made efforts to stop it. Today the Easter experience is being manifested by the life examples of the German Chancellor Angela Merkel, the German people, and people of European Union nations, all who are supporting the migrant refugees, Salah Farah, a Muslim teacher who died in Kenya shielding Christians during a bus attack, the examples the truck drivers and the support staff who risk their lives to send food items and medicine to people in war torn zones of this troubled world and all who are making genuine efforts to stop the conflicts and help the traumatized victim of the global wars.

The promulgation of the Easter experience as a forty day event that encouraged people to do good deeds is an obstacle to Jesus's public exhibition of the miracle of human creation. First, performance of good works without the experience of Jesus' Kingdom of God is for the camera and publicity. Second, the resurrection of Christ, a significant scene in the final event in the epic miracle of life, is a confirmation that our "life is hid with Christ." (Colossians 3:3) Our Easter experience should be the desire to be with risen Christ, striving to obey all His commandments and, manifesting our experience of His Kingdom of God every day and not just during the Easter period. In essence, Easter Experience is the experience of Jesus's Kingdom of God as an active participant in the everlasting miracle of human creation. It is an experience of the earthly phase of eternal life.

The resurrection of Jesus unfolded and exposed the deep mysteries of His Kingdom of God. As the power of that Kingdom propelled Him, to unleash its power in creation as was demonstrated by Him through His death and resurrection, what was once considered an inscrutable mystery of the cross unfolded, revealing its glory. Today we celebrate that glory as Easter. To embark on our creative journey without the power of Jesus's Kingdom of God is like sailing an uncharted sea. Jesus's Kingdom of God carries with it the Spirit of the truth, justice, harmony, love that extended to the enemy, humility, compassion for the world and all the blessings of the beatitudes, providing in essence, the tools for our journey to be the prototype of what was revealed on Easter

> *Therefore let no man glory in men. For all things are yours; whether Paul, or Apollos, or Cephas, or the world, or life, or death, or things present, or things to come; all are yours; and ye are Christ's; and Christ is God's.*

Paul. 1 Corinthians 3:21-23

A guided insight into the mysteries of Easter revealed the mystery of life and human experience of it that is rooted in Jesus's Kingdom of God, His miracle of human creation, the new God, the Father that Jesus introduced to the world, who Jesus is, who we are, why we are here and our glorious destiny. It is a guarantee of Jesus's kingdom of God (the Spirit of the Father through Christ in action) within the human souls and our participation in the journey of eternal life as demonstrated in the epic miracle. This is the true glory of Easter! This is the mystery that the cross held back for more than two thousand years. This is the encrypted mystery of Easter that I recovered from the Gospel literature. This is the revealed mystery that calls for Easter celebration! Paul spoke of this mystery: "Even the mystery which hath been hid from ages and from generations, but now is made manifest to his saints: To whom God would make known what is the riches of the glory of this mystery among the Gentiles; which is Christ in you, the hope of glory." (Colossians 1:26-27)

What is not stressed during the Easter services is that the knowledge of what Easter means carries with it an enormous task for humans: the quest to have real knowledge of the Father who sent Jesus Christ, the desire to enter into Jesus's Kingdom of God, experience and manifest it, public proclamation of the true meaning of Easter to all who are willing to have that knowledge, love for all mankind that extends to the enemy, compassion, justice, peace, elimination of all wars including hatred, jealousy, hypocrisy, racism, bigotry, greed and selfishness. This would be your gift of Easter, not the egg or Easter baskets, to your children and to humanity. The children may ask you: "where is this risen Christ that we may develop and have the Easter experience with Him?" Tell them Chancellor Angela Merkel found Him on the faces of all the migrant refugees that came to the German boarders and took more than one million of them into her country. Read the story of the Good Samaritan to them before you go to Church on Easter. Show them the pictures of the forgotten population in refugee camps. The risen Christ is everywhere. Find the risen Christ for your children, even if you have to skip that Easter sunrise service and the practice of finding the hidden Easter eggs. Decorate and fill their Easter baskets with the precious ornaments of the risen Christ: humility, love, mercy, care of the poor, compassion and forgiveness.

Suffer little children to come unto me, and forbid them not; for such is the Kingdom of God.

---Luke 18:16

My little children let us not love in word, neither in tongue; but in deed and in truth.

---1 John 3:18

For we are his workmanship, created in Christ Jesus unto good works, which God hath before ordained that we should walk in them.

---Ephesians 2:10

Enjoy the glory of Easter that was revealed!

CHAPTER 10

POST-RESURRECTION SCENES OF JESUS'S MIRACLE OF LIFE

This epiphany is not to prove Jesus's resurrection. Mary Magdalene was the first to see the rise Christ. (Mark 16:9; John 20: 11-17) Simon Peter was the first apostle to see Him after His resurrection. (Luke 24:34)

Scene 1

Encounter with Cleopas and His Companions. (Luke 24:13-31)

And, behold, two of them went that same day to a village called Emmaus, which was from Jerusalem about threescore furlongs. And they talked together of all these things which had happened. And it came to pass, that, while they communed together and reasoned, Jesus Himself drew near, and went with them. But their eyes were holden that they should not know Him. And He said unto them, what manner of communications are these that ye have one to another, as ye walk, and are sad? And the one of them, whose name was Cleopas, answering said unto Him, Art thou only a stranger in Jerusalem, and hast not known the things which are come to pass there in these days? And He said unto them, what things? And they said unto Him, Concerning Jesus of Nazareth, which was a prophet mighty in deed and word before God and all the people: And how the chief priests and our rulers delivered Him to be condemned to death, and have crucified Him. But we trusted that it had been He which should have redeemed Israel: and beside all this, today is the third day since these things were done. Yea, and certain women also of our company made us astonished, which were early at the sepulchre; And when they found not His body, they came, saying, that they had also seen a vision of angels, which said that He was alive. And certain of them which were with us went to the sepulchre, and found it even so as the women had said: but Him they saw not. And they drew nigh unto the village, whither they went: and He made as though he would have gone further. But they constrained Him, saying, Abide with us: for it is toward evening, and the day is far spent. And He went in to tarry with them. And it came to pass, as He sat at meat with them, He took bread, and blessed it, and brake, and gave to them. And their eyes were opened, and they knew Him; and He vanished out of their sight.

---Luke 24: 13-24; 28-31

Scene 2

First Appearance of the Risen Christ to the other Apostles
On the same day of His resurrection, Jesus appeared to the apostles. Thomas was not present.

And they (Cloepas and his friends) *told what things were done in the way, and how He* (Jesus) *was known of them in breaking of bread. And as they thus spake, Jesus himself stood in the midst of them, and saith unto them, "Peace be unto you." But they were terrified and affrighted, and supposed that they had seen a spirit. And He said unto them, why are ye troubled? And why do thoughts arise in your hearts? Behold my hands and my feet, that it is I myself.*

---Luke 24: 35-39

Scene 3

Second Appearance to the Apostles.
When the news of the resurrection of Jesus was reported to the apostle Thomas, he doubted it. He was not present when the risen Christ appeared to the other apostles. On the eighth day after His resurrection, the apostles were having a meal together, and Thomas was with them. Though the doors were locked, Jesus came and stood among them and said, "Peace be with you." He looked at Thomas and said: "Put your finger here, and see my hands. Reach out your hand and put it into my side. Stop doubting and believe."

Thomas said to Him: "My Lord and my God."

When Thomas saw the resurrected Christ with His own eyes, he recognized immediately the divine sovereignty of his Master.

Scene 4

Third Appearance to the Apostles by the Sea of Tiberius. (John 21:1-23)
During that encounter, the apostle John observed that: "It is the Lord," and Jesus asked Peter to: "Feed my Sheep."

Scene 5

Fourth Appearance to the Apostles on Mount Olives-East Side of Jerusalem. (Luke 24:44-49)
Jesus instructed them not to leave Jerusalem.

> *And, behold, I send the promise of my Father upon you: but tarry ye in the city of Jerusalem, until ye be endued with power from on high.*

---Jesus

Saint Paul gave an overview of the post-resurrection of Jesus in his first letter to the Corinthians.

> *For I delivered unto you first of all that which I also received, how that Christ died for our sins according to the scriptures; And that he was buried, and that he rose again the third day according to the scriptures: And that he was seen of Cephas, then of the twelve: After that, he was seen of above five hundred brethren at once; of whom the greater part remain unto this present, but some are fallen asleep. After that, he was seen of James; then of all the apostles. And last of all he was seen of me also, as of one born out of due time.*

---1 Corinthians 15:3-8

CHAPTER 11

ASCENSION OF CHRIST AT BETHANY, NEAR MOUNT OLIVES

And he led them out as far as to Bethany, and he lifted up
his hands, and blessed them. And it came to pass, while
he blessed them, he was parted from them, and carried
up into heaven. And they worshipped him, and returned
to Jerusalem with great joy: And were continually in the
temple, praising and blessing God. Amen.

—Luke 24:50-53

We do not know where Jesus spent all His time or where He slept during the forty days and nights from the morning of His resurrection to the day He ascended to heaven. We know that after His first appearance to Mary Magdalene, He went to present Himself to His Father: "Touch me not," Jesus said to Mary, "for I am not yet ascended to my Father; but go to my brethren, and say unto them, I ascend unto my Father, and your Father; and to my God, and your God." (John 20:17) However, the risen Jesus Christ came back that day and appeared to His apostles. The apostle Thomas was not present. However, after eight days, Jesus appeared again to all of them and allowed Thomas to touch Him. Subsequently, Jesus manifested to many people during that period. Jesus had planned to ascend to heaven from Bethany and did not disclose that information. He wanted only the elect followers given to Him by the Father to witness His ascension to heaven. Jesus did not want people to camp out at Bethany, waiting for Him to appear again, as they did after Lazarus was resurrected. Bethany harbored the last earthly footprints of the resurrected Jesus Christ!

Jesus said to the apostles, "All power is given unto me in heaven and on earth. Go ye therefore and teach all nations, baptizing them in the name of the Father and of the Son, and of the Holy Ghost: teaching them to observe all things whatsoever I have commanded you; and lo, I am with you always, even unto the end of the world." (Matthew 28:18-20) It was reported that while Jesus was speaking to them, He was carried into heaven.

I came forth from the Father, and am come into the world; again I leave the world, and go to the Father.

---John16:28

And no man hath ascended up to heaven, but He that came down from heaven.

---John 3:13

If any man serve me, let him follow me; and where I am, there shall also my servant be; if any man serve me, him will my Father honor.

---John 12:26

CHAPTER 12

THE PROMISED GIFT OF THE HOLY SPIRIT OF CHRIST AND PENTECOST

The Audience.

His apostles, the Jews and proselytes in Jerusalem, Roman soldiers and officers in Jerusalem, visitors that came for the Passover feast-Parthians, Cretes and Arabians, Medes, Elamites, people from Mesopotamia, Judaea, Cappadocia, Pontus, Asia, Phrygia, Pamphylia, Egypt, parts of Libya about Cyrene and Rome.

> *But the Comforter, which is the Holy Ghost, whom the Father will send in my name, he shall teach you all things, and bring to your remembrance, whatsoever I have said unto you."*

> ---John 14:26

> *And, being assembled together with them, commanded them that they should not depart from Jerusalem, but wait for the promise of the Father, which, saith he, ye have heard of me. For John truly*

baptized with water; but ye shall be baptized with the Holy Ghost not many days hence.

---Acts 1:4-5

Jesus Christ and His Father, kept their promise. On the day of Pentecost, when the Spirit of the risen Jesus Christ manifested again, the apostles received the promised power from Heaven. "And when the day of the Pentecost was fully come, they (the apostles) were all with one accord in one place. And suddenly there came a sound from heaven as of a rushing mighty wind, and it filled the entire house where they were sitting. And there appeared unto them cloven tongues like as of fire, and it filled the entire house where they were sitting. And there appeared unto them cloven tongues like as of fire, and it sat upon each of them. And they were filled with the Holy Ghost, and began to speak with other tongues, as the Spirit gave them utterance." And there were dwelling at Jerusalem Jews, devout men, out of every nation under heaven. Now when this was noised abroad, the multitude came together and was confounded, because that every man heard them speak in his own language. And they were all amazed and marveled, saying one to another, Behold, are not all these which speak Galileans? And how hear we every man in our own tongue, wherein we were born? (Acts 2:1-8)

We have read it over and over again, how on the day of the Pentecost, after they had received the Holy Ghost, the apostles who spoke only Galilean language, addressed the audience and everyone understood the message in their own language. If it happens today, the Africans will hear that message in their own language, the British in English, the South Americans in Spanish, the Russians, French and the Germans in their own native languages. It was a new experience for the apostles. It never happened before in the history of mankind. Jesus could have given them a spiritual gift that would make them disappear in hostile situations with the Jewish authorities. He could endow them with the power of transfiguration. Have you ever wondered why that promised gift was the ability to speak languages which they had never learned?

The apostles had received the great commission from their Master, "Go ye into the entire world, and preach the gospel to every creature," (Mark 16:15) "teaching them to observe all things whatsoever I have commanded you." (Matthew 28:20) The apostles were correctly identified on the day of Pentecost as the men who spoke Galilean. If that was the only language they had to use to disseminate Jesus's message without the gift of the Holy Spirit, many people would not understand them. It would not be enough to express the vast information of what they had learned and witnessed. The problem was real.

> *But when they shall lead you, and deliver you up, take no thought*
> *beforehand what ye shall speak, neither do ye premeditate: but what-*
> *soever shall be given you in that hour, that speak ye: for it is not ye*
> *that speak, but the Holy Ghost.*

---Mark 13:11

On the day of Pentecost, Jesus endowed the apostles with His Holy Spirit that perpetually spoke for them when they were brought before Judges and the Jewish authorities. It enabled them to intelligently speak in many languages. People of other nations understood them as they proclaimed the vital information on what they learned and observed on the words and works of Christ. By this endowment of His Holy Spirit, the promised gift from His Father, Jesus again manifested the infinite power of His Kingdom of God and used the apostles in that model demonstration. This is the mystery of Pentecost.

Verily I say unto you, that there be some of them that stand here, which shall not taste of death, till they have seen the Kingdom of God come with power.

---Mark 9:1

What happened on the day of Pentecost to the apostles, fifty days after the ascension of Christ, provided one of the finest scenes in Jesus's epic miracle of human creation. An event like that never occurred in the recorded history of mankind. That miracle did not end with the resurrection and ascension of Christ. That metaphysical drama of the cross that manifested the power of Jesus's Kingdom of God in its trajectory of human creation extended its tentacles to the spiritual events on the day of Pentecost. What was thought to be a historical tragedy at Golgotha was indeed a channel though which mankind would have a glimpse into the evolutionary process of human creation and into the spiritual world of Christ and His Father. It provided mankind with permanent power of Jesus's Kingdom of God for our participation in the earthly stages of the miracle of human creation. The last scene of the epic miracle that manifested on the day of Pentecost, marked the moment in the history of mankind when the power of the glorified risen Christ flowed into human souls, implanting His Spirits to enable us to perpetually pass through the gate of death in our journey to eternal. Jesus used His apostles for that infinite display of the proof of the power of His Kingdom of God and in doing so, prepared them for worldwide dissemination of His words and works. These are the deep mysteries of Jesus Kingdom of God that powered all the events, revealing along its trajectory, deeper mysteries of Golgotha! My dear readers, this vital knowledge matters for everything we do, do not leave this planet

Earth without "Christ in me." The best of what Jesus Christ and His Father planned for us is yet to be revealed when the time is fulfilled.

The fulfillment of that promise from the Father marked the last scene in the exhibition of Jesus's everlasting miracle of the ultimate human creation. Its exhibition provided mankind with the proof of the existence of the Father, His love for all mankind and the power of Jesus's Kingdom of God. By the fulfillment of that promise, the blurred picture of the invisible Father, who planned, controlled and directed the miracle, became a vibrant illuminating image. It revealed a universal living and true God who belongs to the world and not just to those who call themselves Christians. The Father, who kept His promise without killing anyone or by annihilating the enemy, can only be a real living true God.

Neither pray I for these alone, but for them also which shall believe in me through their word; That they all may be one; as thou, Father, art in me, and I in thee, that they also may be one in us: that the world may believe that thou hast sent me. And the glory which thou gavest me I have given them; that they may be one, even as we are one: I in them, and thou in me, that they may be made perfect in one; and that the world may know that thou hast sent me, and hast loved them, as thou hast loved me. Father, I will that they also, whom thou hast given me, be with me where I am; that they may behold my glory, which thou hast given me: for thou lovedst me before the foundation of the world. O righteous Father, the world hath not known thee: but I have known thee, and these have known that thou hast sent me. And I have declared unto them thy name, and will declare it: that the love wherewith thou hast loved me may be in them, and I in them.

The authenticity and the divine origin of the above Jesus's words and many of His other words and deeds were validated by the fulfillment of the promised gift of the Holy Ghost from His Father. We no longer need to ask Jesus: who are you or where do you come from? Jesus had said, "I proceeded forth and came from God, neither came I of myself but He sent me." (John 8:42) We no longer have to doubt His authentic words on His divine origin. We do not need to go to Heaven to trace His origin. Be careful of the words put into His mouth. We no longer need to ask Him: are you also a God? We no longer need to ask Him to reveal the Kingdom of God that came in terms that we can understand. We no longer need to ask Him: are you a Creator also? The fulfillment of the promise provided proof of the authenticity of His words that He is the Lord of Resurrection, an invaluable companion in the transcendental transformation of the human soul in its journey for eternal life.

Then answered Jesus and said unto them, Verily, verily, I say unto you, The Son can do nothing of himself, but what he seeth the Father do: for what things soever he doeth, these also doeth the Son likewise. For the Father loveth the Son and sheweth him all things that himself doeth: and he will shew him greater works than these that ye may marvel. For as the Father raiseth up the dead, and quickeneth them; even so the Son quickeneth whom he will. Verily, verily, I say unto you, He that heareth my word, and believeth on him that sent me, hath everlasting life, and shall not come into condemnation; but is passed from death unto life. Verily, verily, I say unto you, the hour is coming, and now is, when the dead shall hear the voice of the Son of God: and they that hear shall live. For as the Father hath life in himself; so hath he given to the Son to have life in himself; and hath given him authority to execute judgment also, because he is the Son of man. Marvel not at this: for the hour is coming, in the which all that are in the graves shall hear his voice, And shall come forth; they that have done good, unto the resurrection of life; and they that have done evil, unto the resurrection of damnation.

Jesus. John 5: 19-21; 24-29

By the recreation of Himself as demonstrated in that everlasting miracle, and as displayed in the final scene on the day of Pentecost, Jesus bounded all the divine element of creation and catapulted that infinite creative authority and power to Himself and to His Father. Jesus's everlasting miracle of the earthly stages of human creation provided the evidence that the God revealed by Moses in the book of Genesis is not the Creator of human beings.

We no longer need to ask Jesus: Where is thy Father? This Father, who kept His promise, sent Jesus to the world.

I know Him, for I am from Him, and He hath sent me.

---Jesus. John 7:29

I am not of this world.

---Jesus

It was Jesus who predetermined and broke the news on what His Father will do. That His Father will send the Holy Spirit in "my" name. His Father did it! The Holy Spirit, also called the Comforter that was sent by His Father is the glorified Spirit of the risen Christ. The exhibition of that last scene in Jesus's everlasting miracle of life, provided mankind with evidence of the glorious destiny of the prototype of the spiritual new creature that was revealed by the resurrection of Jesus. That glorious destiny would end in the place where the fulfilled promise of the Father originated. The gift of the promised Holy Spirit provided evidence that what Jesus said about human life and His authority on eternal life were true. It gave us a proof that heaven exists, and the confidence that we can ascend to it.

Timing was very important in the final execution of the miracle of human creation. The crucifixion of Jesus was carried out during the week of the Passover feast. The Father and Jesus Christ wanted the people who came to Jerusalem from many parts of the world to witness that glorious event. The final scene of Jesus everlasting miracle of human life must also be given at a time when people from many parts of the world would come again to Jerusalem for an occasion to be spectators of the great miracle. The Father and His Son waited until the time was fulfilled. The Pentecost feast, a festival of thanks for the harvest, and remembered as the time when the Law was given to the Israelites on Sinai was celebrated on the fiftieth day from the Passover feast. Jesus had told His apostles not to leave Jerusalem and to wait for the promise of the Father-the baptism of the Holy Ghost.

But ye shall receive power, after that the Holy Ghost is come upon you: and ye shall be witnesses unto me both in Jerusalem, and in all Judaea, and in Samaria, and unto the uttermost part of the earth.

---Acts 1:8

The glorified Spirit of risen Christ that would guide the human soul in all its future evolutionary creative processes, was released in full power on the day of Pentecost. The ultimate power of Jesus's Kingdom of God in that final scene of His epic miracle of life, manifested again as was demonstrated by the apostles on the day of Pentecost. What happened on the day of Pentecost, were events that empowered the souls of the apostles and since then, has continued to empower the souls of all that believe in Jesus Christ and His Father, to participate in Jesus's Kingdom of God and strive for its objectives and goals. The core element in that Kingdom is the Spirit of Christ. All His miracles, including the everlasting miracle of life, were executed by the power of Jesus's Kingdom of God. The introduction of the concept of Trinity would suggest that Jesus's Kingdom of God ended with His ascension to heaven and that another Spirit called the Holy Ghost was sent down by His Father, to spiritualize the apostles on the day of Pentecost. In essence, it would seem that there are two Kingdoms of God-one powered by the Spirit of Christ before His death and the other by the Holy Ghost after His resurrection. The eyewitnesses saw and talked to the risen Christ. Paul heard His voice on his way to Damascus. If the Holy Ghost is another Spirit, we are yet to see Him or hear His voice. There is only one Kingdom of God that was proclaimed by Christ. It was the same Holy Spirit of the risen Jesus Christ that came on the day of Pentecost.

The fulfillment of that promise gave humankind confidence that when we pray, that we have direct access to the glorified Spirit of Christ and His Father. Its conception was spiritual. Its dispensation was from heaven. It opened a door to all mankind who are able to receive that glorified Spirit of Jesus that came back on the day of Pentecost, to enter and see what had been hidden from wise men and the Prophets, but revealed only to the apostles. It was revealed to everyone on the day of Pentecost, but few people comprehended it. Its manifestations since that Spirit was endowed to humankind on the day of Pentecost have been spectacular and extraordinary. It enabled the apostles to speak intelligently in many languages and everyone under-stood them. It threatened the very foundations of Judaism that prompted the Jews and their leaders to take fatal actions against the apostles, Paul and others who were proclaiming what that promise accomplished. At first, the Romans could not tolerate it. However, empowered by the Spirit of that risen Christ they received on the day of Pentecost, the apostles with Paul and oth-ers invaded the Greco-Roman Empire. When it was all over, the great Roman Empire subjected itself to Christianity; their Gods and Goddesses were silenced and their temples destroyed. The Jewish Temple at Jerusalem was also destroyed.

On the day of the Pentecost, there were one hundred and twenty people who believed in Jesus Christ. Today, there are more than two billion Christians! Jesus's everlasting miracle is still revealing some of its mysteries and will continue to do so to the end of time. That gift of the Holy Ghost-the glorified Spirit of the risen Christ-would live in our hearts forever. It will accomplish and manifest all the divine imprints it carries along with it. With the power of its Kingdom, we can imitate the apostles by activating that Kingdom within us. If we obey all the commandments of Jesus Christ, we will, like the apostles on the day of Pentecost, obtain the gift of the Holy Spirit that will help us understand and remind us of the teachings of Christ, allow us to be benefactors of what all that Jesus's epic miracle revealed, and empower us to speak in tongues that people of other languages can understand. Today, the façade of speaking in tongues translated into mystic speeches nobody understands. This false imitation of the experience of the apostles and Paul is an impassable barrier to the understanding of the nature of the Holy Spirit.

"I have yet many things to say unto you, but you cannot hear them now."

(John 16:12)

Jesus still has many things to reveal to us. His policy of secrecy and silence as directed by the Father and His refusal to fully reveal Himself still persists. It would seem that this policy made the interpretation of who Jesus is and what He accomplished in Jerusalem and at Golgotha imperceptible and elusive. But Jesus told His apostles that "there is nothing covered that shall not be revealed; and hid, that shall not be known." (Matthew 10:26) I believe that what I have recovered from Jesus's words and works are just a few pebbles from the ocean of infinite mystery. I am inspired from all that I have decoded from Jesus's everlasting miracle of human life that revealed the true meaning of Easter and the infinite power of Jesus's Kingdom of God. I am amazed how it ended with the sound from heaven and with the appearance of "cloven tongues like of fire that first filled the house, and then sat upon each one of them."

If any man serve me, let him follow me; and where I am, there shall also my servant be; if any man serve me, him will my Father honor.

---John 12:26

Jesus's everlasting miracle of the earthly stages of human creation had ended. But its experiences in human souls, as we embark on the journey to our destiny are without end. The power of the knowledge of the Father and Jesus Christ and the earthy life of the human soul and its destiny is priceless. The promises of earthly glory, materialistic heaven on earth, and the coming of Christ to this planet to take us to heaven is now naïve and irrelevant. The power of Jesus's everlasting miracle of human creation, rooted in His Kingdom of God, is within us. Jesus's words and His miracle of life show how easily we can get it and use that power to move along all the earthly stages of human creation as demonstrated by Christ. First we must possess and activate that Kingdom and be willing to be participants in our creation as to experience its mighty creative power and its blessings.

Do not be afraid to enter into Jesus's Kingdom of God. That Kingdom of God is the power that moves all human creative activities to perfection, revealing along this trajectory, some of its deep mysteries. It is the underlying divine element in all human life. It originated from His Father. It is an indestructible, non-erasable spiritual thread that unites all mankind, manifesting its infinite power in human creation as was demonstrated by Jesus in the everlasting miracle of earthly stages of human creation. We are not yet fully created. The Holy Spirit of the risen Christ that was given to the apostles on the day of Pentecost is within every one of us today. Activate it now and be a participant of the new human spirits that the Father and Jesus Christ are creating.

Jesus, who used Himself as a model in His miracle of human creation-the miracle of life-provided us with proofs that life is real and has intrinsic value; that His Father is a living God and a Creator; that He is also a God and a Creator! My inspiration is based on my optimism that mankind will use the vital information in this book to move forward in a completely different direction that would benefit all mankind and guide us as a unified community toward our glorious destiny as revealed in Jesus's everlasting miracle of human life.

THE CAST
The Architect and Director of the Epic Miracle of Life:
God, the Father of Jesus Christ (Present in Spirit)
The Principal Actor and Executor:
Jesus Christ
Leading Actor and Actress in Supporting Role:
Joseph and Mary, the parents of Jesus Christ
Special Agent behind the Scene:
The apostle Judas Iscariot
Other Actors and Actresses in Supporting Roles:
Other eleven apostles, Joseph of Arimathaea, Nicodemus and Mary Magdalene.

The Jews:
Jewish people in Palestine, Jewish Diaspora, the Jewish authorities (the Jewish Priests, the scribes and other members of the Sanhedrin). The sick people Jesus cured. The five thousand people Jesus fed with five loaves of bread and two fishes. The Jewish 'soldiers of fortune' who were give large sum of money to bear false witness against Jesus. The people of Cana in Galilee where

Jesus performed the first miracle. Cleopas and his companions. Bartimeus, the son of Timoeus, Zaccheus of Jericho,

The Romans:
Governor Pontius Pilate. The Roman soldiers and officers. The Roman soldiers who put Jesus on the cross,

The Greeks:
Certain Greeks who, a few days earlier, were introduced to Jesus by Philip and Andrew

Others:
Simon, a Cyrenian, who was compelled to help Jesus carry His cross to Golgotha. The Gentile who came to Jerusalem for the Pentecost. The Samaritan woman Jesus asked for water. The people of Palestine who were not Jews. Some of the people who were at Golgotha, when Jesus was crucified. All other people not in the above list, to whom Jesus revealed Himself after His resurrection, before His ascension.

BIBLIOGRAPHY

Adams, Marilyn M. *Horrendous Evils and the Goodness of God*. Ithaca: Cornell UP, 1999.

Armstrong Karen. *A History of God*. Ballantine Book. NY. USA 1993

Anderson, Hugh, ed. *Jesus*. Englewood Cliffs: Prentice-Hall, Inc., 1967.

Anderson Paul. The Riddles of the Fourth Gospel. Fortress Press. Minneapolis. USA 2011

Aulen, Gustaf. *Dag Hammarskjold's White Book*. Philadelphia: Fortress Press, 1969.

Barclay, William. *Jesus as They Saw Him*. Grand Rapids: William B. Eerdmans Company, 1962.

Beasley Murray. *Jesus and the Kingdom of God*. The Paternoster Press. UK 1986

Bornkamm, Günther. *Jesus of Nazareth*. Trans. Irene McLuskey and Fraser McLuskey. Minneapolis: Fortress P, 1995.

Jesus the Human life of God. Forward Movt. Publication. Ohio. USA. 1987

Borsch Fredrick. *God's Parable*. The Westminister Press Philadelphia. USA 1975

Bright John. *The Kingdom of God*. Abingdon Press. USA 1953

Brown, Raymond E. *The Death of the Messiah*. Vol. 2. New York: Doubleday, 1994.

Burton, Trochmorton Jr. *Gospel Parallels*. Nashville: Thomas Nelson Publishers, 1979.

Candlish James. *The Kingdom of God Biblically and Historically considered*. HardPress Publishers. Miami, Fl. USA. 1882

Carus, Paul. *The Gospel of Buddha*. Chicago: Carus Company, 2004.

Cooper, Terry D. *Dimensions of Evil*. Minneapolis: Fortress P, 2007.

Davies, Oliver, trans. *Eckhart: Selected Writings*. London: Penguin Books, 1994.1961

Davis Stephen et al *The Resurrection* Oxford University Press. USA 1997

Dimont Max. Jews, God and History. Signet Classics. (Penguin Group) USA. 2004

Dodd C. H. *The Parables of the Kingdom*. Charles Scribner;s & Sons. USA

Donahue John. *The Gospel in Parables*. Fortress Press. USA 1990

Dych William. *Thy Kingdom come*. Herder and Herder Books. USA 1999

Emerson, Harry Fosdick. *The Man from Nazareth*. New York: Harper and Brothers, 1949.

Enumah, Festus. MD. *The Innocent Blood and Judas Iscariot*. Guardian Books: Canada, 2002.

Enumah Festus MD. *The Father's Business and the Spiritual Cross*. Published in Charleston. USA 2014

Fallows, Samuel Rt. Rev. *Bible Encyclopedia and Scriptural Dictionary*. Chicago: The Howard-Severance Company, 1907.

Ferguson Sinclair. *The Holy Spirit*. InterVasity Press. ILL. USA. 1996

Fite Warner. *Jesus the Man*. Harvard University Press. USA. 1946

Forde, Gerhard. *On Being a Theologian of the Cross*. Grand Rapids: William B. Eerdmans Comp., 1997.

Fosdick Harry. *The Man from Nazareth*. Harper and Brothers. NY. USA 1949

Fuellenbach John. *The Kingdom of God*. Orbis Books. NY. 1995

Goguel, Maurice. *Jesus and the Origin of Christianity.* Vols. 1 & 2. New York: Harper Torchbooks, 1960.

Gordon, D. Kaufman. *In Face of Mystery.* Cambridge: Harvard University Press, 1995.

Gordon Kaufman *Jesus and Creativity.* Fortress Press. USA 2006

Gunton C. E. *Christ and Creation.* William Eerdmans Publishing, USA 1992

Häring, Bernard. *The Law of Christ.* Trans. Edwin G. Kaiser. Westminster: The Newman P, 1963.

Harnack, Adolf. *What is Christianity?* New York: Harper & Brothers Publishers, 1957.

Harnack Adolf. *Marcion and the Gospel of Alien God.* Wipf and Stock Publishers. USA 2007

Hengel, Martin. *Crucifixion.* Philadelphia: Fortress P, 1977.

Hick, John. *Death and Eternal Life.* Louisville: Westminster/John Knox P, 1994.

Hick John *Evil and the God of Love.* Palgrave Macmillian Press USA 1977

Hoenig, Sidney B. *The Great Sanhedrin.* Philadelphia: Bloch Publishing Co. 1953.

Holland Henry Scott. *God's City and the coming of the Kingdom.* Longmans, Green & Co
NY. USA 1987

The Holy Bible, Original King James Version. Gordonsville: Dugan Publishers Inc., 1985.

Jackson Samuel Macauley. *The new Schaff-Herzog Encyclopedia of Religious Knowledge.*
Baker Book House. Grand Rapid. Michigan. USA 1950

Jeremias Joachin *Jerusalem in Times of Jesus.* Philadelphia: Fortress Press, 1969.

Jeremias, Joachim..*The Parables of Jesus.* Prentice-Hall. USA 1963

Kaufman Gordon *God the Problem.* Harvard University Press. USA. 1972

Kaufmann Walter (Introducer) *Religion from Tolstoy to Camus.* Harper Torch Books. N.Y. 1961

Kim Kirsteen. *The Holy Spirit in the world.* Orbis Books. NY. USA 2007

Kittay, Eva F. *Metaphor.* Oxford: Clarendon P, 1989

Ladd George. *The Gospel of the Kingdom.* William B. Eerdmans Publishers. USA

Lakoff, George, and Mark Johnson. *Metaphors We Live By.* Chicago: University of Chicago P, 1980.

Linwood Urban *A short history of Christian thoughts.* Oxford University Press 1995.

Lockyer, Herbert. *All the Messiah Prophecies of the Bible.* Grand Rapids: Zondervan Publishing House, 1960.

McConkie Jeseph et al. *The Holy Spirit.* Bookcraft. Utah. USA 1989

McInerny, D. Q. *Being Logical.* New York: Random House, 2004.

Meeks, Wayne A., ed. *The Writings of St. Paul.* New York: W. W. Norton & Company, Inc., 1972.

Moltmann Jurgen. *God in Creation.* Fortress Press. Minneapolis. USA 1993

Nelson-Pallmeyer. *Jesus against Christianity.* Harrisburg, Penn.: Trinity Press International, 2001.

Norman Beck. *Mature Christianity in the 21ˢᵗ Century.* Crossroad. NY, USA 1994

Nuss Donald. The Anatomies of God, the Bible, and Religion

O'Malley Williams. *God the oldest Question.* Loyola Press. ILL. USA 2000

Pelikan, Jaroslav. *Jesus Through the Centuries.* New York: Harper & Row, 1985.

Pink Arthur. *The Beatitudes and the Lord's Prayer.* Baker Books. USA 1979

Richards, Lawrence O. *The Word Bible Handbook.* Waco: Word, Inc., 1982.

Sanday, William. *The International Critical Commentary on the Holy Scripture of the Old and New Testaments.* New York: Charles Scribners Sons, 1920.

Schillebeeckx, Edward. *Jesus: An experiment in Christology.* New York: Seabury, 1979.

Sheen, Fulton J. *Life of Christ.* New York: Image Books Doubleday. 1958.

Schweitzer Albert *The mystery of the Kingdom of God.* Dodd, Mead Publishers. USA 1914

Simkhovitch, Vladimir. *Toward the Understanding of Jesus.* New York: The MacMillan Company,1925.

Spong John Shelby. *Liberating the Gospels.* HarperSan Francisco. USA 1996

Stott, John. *The Cross of Christ.* Downers Grove: InterVarsity P, 1986.

Thompson Marianne Meye. *The Promise of the Father.* Westminister John Knox Press. USA. 2000

Tolstoy Leo. *The Kingdom of God is within you.* University of Nebraska Press USA. 1984

Townshend, George. *The Heart of the Gospel.* London: Templar Printing Works, 1939.

Toynbee, Arnold. *The Crucible of Christianity.* New York: The World Publishing Company, 1969.

Wesley John. *The nature of the Kingdom.* Bethany House Publishers. USA. 1979.

Wilson, Ian. *Jesus: The Evidence.* New York: Harper Collins Publishers, 1984.

Wood, et al. *Immanuel Kant: Religion within the Boundaries of Mere Reason And Other Writings.* Cambridge: Cambridge UP, 1998.

Dr. Festus Enumah has arranged for part of his share of the proceeds from all his books to be donated to Samuel A. Enumah Africancer Foundation, www.africancer.org, a public, charitable nonprofit 501(c) (3) corporation registered in the state of Georgia, USA. The objective of the foundation is to help develop and build the infrastructure in sub-Saharan Africa for cancer control services, focusing on cancer education, prevention, early detection and treatment. The aim of the foundation is to help reduce the deaths from cancer and improve cancer patients' quality of life.

ABOUT THE AUTHOR

Festus Enumah, MD, graduated from the University of Ibadan Medical School and Government College, both in Nigeria. A board-certified surgeon with many years in practice, Enumah trained at Cook County Hospital in Chicago and at the University of Texas M. D. Anderson Cancer Center in Houston. He is married to Lois Bronersky-Enumah, who is also a board-certified family physician. They have four children.

Enumah is also the author of *The Innocent Blood and Judas Iscariot* and *The Father's Business and the Spiritual Cross.*

Enumah's special medical interests include breast cancer, gastrointestinal and chest tumors, preventative and early cancer detection, and stem-cell tumor biology. He's the founder and president of the Samuel A. Enumah Africancer Foundation, a US nonprofit that is working to build sustainable cancer detection and treatment in sub-Saharan Africa and aims to develop a model that will serve patients regardless of socio-economic status. Enumah and his wife have also worked in a volunteer capacity in Nigeria, where they ran a free medical clinic.

Enumah enjoys a variety of sports, including golf and tennis, and he collects Bibles and rare books on Christianity.

www.ingramcontent.com/pod-product-compliance
Lightning Source LLC
Chambersburg PA
CBHW031321040426
42443CB00005B/174